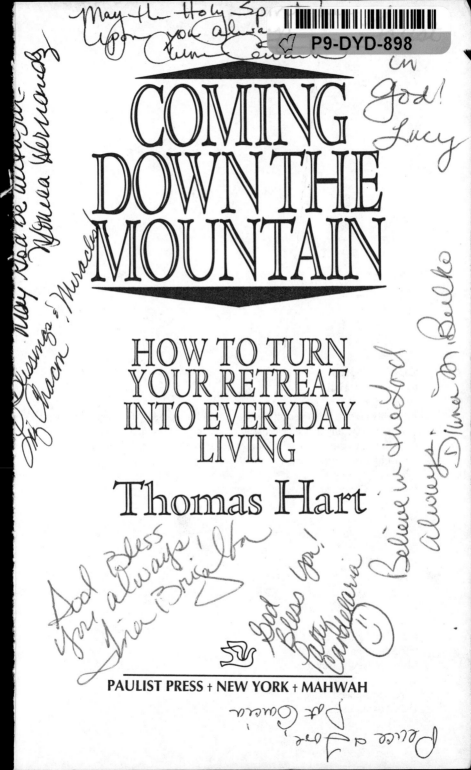

COMING DOWN THE MOUNTAIN

HOW TO TURN YOUR RETREAT INTO EVERYDAY LIVING

Thomas Hart

PAULIST PRESS + NEW YORK + MAHWAH

Library of Congress Cataloging-in-Publication Data

Hart, Thomas N.
    Coming down the mountain.

        1. Christian life—1960–   . 2. Retreats.
I. Title.
BV4501.2.H363   1988   248.4   88-2490
ISBN 0-8091-2965-5 (pbk.)

Published by Paulist Press
997 Macarthur Boulevard
Mahwah, New Jersey 07430

Printed and bound in the
United States of America

Contents

iii

Introduction

You just finished a retreat. You feel close to God, and are eager to take your new energy and fresh Christian perspectives out into the world and live that life you so deeply want to live.

This book is written to help you do that. It is a follow-up to your retreat, designed to keep that experience alive and influential in your life. Every day for six weeks it offers you a reflection on some aspect of Christian living, a scripture passage for your prayer, and a task to carry out. All the key relationships of your life are covered—God, yourself, other people, and the world.

The need for some kind of retreat follow-up is clear from experience. For many people, a retreat is a spiritual high that quickly disappears when they reenter the world of daily work and relationships. Within a week or two, the retreat seems very far away and slightly unreal. They cannot quite remember what occurred during it. You do not want that to happen to you. The relationship you have with God is too important. You also know that the Christian life is not something that is meant to be lived just a few days a year in a special quiet setting. Jesus teaches a total way of life, to be lived on a daily basis in the world.

This book addresses the common struggles men and women face as they try to put a Christian vision into practice. It grows out of the many years of work I have done in collaboration with others in pastoral counseling and spiritual direction. You will find here not only suggestions for deepening your relationship with God in prayer, but also ideas for dealing with some of the troublesome areas of life not often addressed in spirituality books. We will discuss loneliness, low self-esteem, difficult relationships, sexuality, grief, and painful memories. We will ponder the difficult questions of why God sometimes seems so far away, and why some awful things happen to us in the world. We will think about how to image God and how to find God's will. We will talk also about play, and peace, and joy.

There are various ways you can use this book. You can read it by yourself a chapter a day, using the scripture passage for your prayer, and carrying out the task which is given to help you put the matter into practice. You could do this the first thing in the morning, or while riding the bus to work. Or you could make it the conclusion of your day and a prelude for the next day. Another way to use the book is to go through it with a group, discussing the reflection and scripture passage together, and then figuring out different ways you could approach the task, possibly even doing some tasks together. Whether you work on your own or in a group, you may not have the time to read a chapter every day. You can slow the pace according to your circumstances. There is value in following the sequence of chapters, as they build on one another, but there is no need to read any of the chapters on the particular day assigned to them.

This book does not have to be tied to a retreat. A retreat is often a significant experience of conversion, and so furnishes a good starting point for doing more sustained work on your faith life. But a person could pick this book up at any time and find it helpful as spiritual reading. It will serve any individual or group of people in almost any circumstances who wish to deepen their relationship with God and live a practical Christian spirituality in daily life.

In the pages that follow, you will explore more fully what it means to live a Christian life and will find practical help for doing it.

Now That Your Retreat Is Over

You have just finished making a retreat. Usually a retreat is a reassuring and renewing experience. During it you enjoy a stronger sense of God's presence and love, feel a comforting and fulfilling closeness, and see your life's purpose and direction much more clearly. Naturally you want to hang on to these things. As a result of what has happened to you, you want to change your life for the better. You leave retreat on a kind of high, determined to live very differently.

Reentry into ordinary existence is often a painful jolt. Back are all your responsibilities, the challenges of daily existence, and the difficulty of some relationships. Not only is it harder than it looked to put your resolutions into practice. Your new clarity of vision seems suddenly to be replaced with the old confusion. And God feels far away.

To minimize the trauma of this transition and to help you preserve the valuable things you have gained on retreat, a couple of reflections might be helpful:

1) *You cannot maintain yourself at your present level of feeling.* Accepting this disappointing fact is the key to peace. You have to let go. Retreat is a privileged time in which God visits you in a special way. The lights go on for a moment, and you see how the land really lies. Then you are returned to ordinary living, which is walking by faith, not by sight. (2 Cor 5:7) There is a parallel in the transfiguration experience Jesus and his disciples had on the mountain. So great were the light and warmth that the disciples wanted to build tents and stay right there. Jesus led them down the mountain, into a crowd of needy people. (Mk 9)

3

2) *It may be a while before you see the effects of the retreat.* Do not expect sudden miracles. You change slowly, even when you would like to change quickly. And you are not usually aware that change is taking place until sometime afterward, when you notice that a former pattern is no longer operating. Your retreat will change something about the way you think or feel or act, over time. But for that to happen, old habits will have to be overcome, and old habits yield slowly. There will be failures while the process is taking place.

3) *You need support.* Is there some way a group of you can meet regularly to keep the retreat alive and growing? Or is there at least one individual, friend or spiritual director, with whom you can share the retreat experience and your attempts to live it out over time? In addition to this support, you will need to do some things yourself to sustain and nourish the retreat perspective—e.g., some regular quiet time with God, some regular scripture or other spiritual reading. Our culture does not generally encourage us in our efforts to be genuinely Christian. We need the support of like-minded friends and of habitual practices to keep faith perspectives fresh.

The experience of retreat is in many ways like the experience of falling in love. Both are wonderful and filled with good feeling. But the intense feelings associated with falling in love do not last. The couple has to make the transition from romantic love to committed love, from an emotional high to the practical matter of loving someone in action day after day. Our relationship with God works much the same way. It too has to undergo the transition from romance to commitment, from grand schemes of the imagination to practical deeds of love in the ordinariness of everyday.

Good News: God will strengthen you to the end, so that you will be blameless on the day of our Lord Jesus. God is faithful, and it was he who called you to fellowship with his Son, Jesus Christ our Lord. (1 Cor 1:8–9)

Christian Action: Choose one important insight about God or yourself from your retreat, and bring it back to mind in any quiet moments you have, for example, when you get up, on your way to work, before going to sleep.

WEEK 1: TUESDAY

Making Your Retreat Last

We talked about making the transition from retreat. Now let us look at some ways you can make your retreat last.

1) *Decide on just one change you are going to make in your life.* Love is shown in deeds, not just in words. When you experience God's love for you, you want to love God in return. How will you do it? Most likely, different ideas came to you on retreat, some actions you were going to stop doing and some you were going to start doing to show more love and to keep the union between God and yourself growing.

If you try to change your whole life at once, you will certainly fail. Pick just one thing. It should be concrete and manageable. For example, you might work on changing the way you relate to just one person in your life. Or you might work on eliminating your habit of procrastination. Focus on that one thing until you feel you have mastered it before moving on to something else.

2) *Expect God to continue to speak to you, but probably in different ways than on the retreat.* The God of the bible is a God who speaks to people, who is not remote but present and involved with our lives. On retreat you probably felt that. Removed from the noise and pressures of your ordinary life, you were quiet and unusually receptive. You could hear far more clearly than you usually do the voice of the God who dwells in your heart as well as the voice of the God who speaks in scripture.

Where does God speak amid the noise and activity of ordinary life, when the heart cannot be so quiet? Expect a shift. Listen for God in the gifts of every day. In the beauty and goodness of the world. In the needs of sisters and brothers. In the moral challenges. In the quiet promptings of your heart. Do not be dismayed if scripture does not seem as eloquent as it did, or if you do not feel God very much. God speaks and acts in many ways. Try to be attentive to the ways God is actually dealing with you now.

3) *Resolve to make a retreat every year or so.* Your experience has taught you that retreat time is special, that pulling back from your ordinary life to seek God directly is exciting and fruitful, that the perspective on your life which you gain on retreat is invaluable. Nothing else works as well, which is why Christian women and men have been going on retreat for centuries, the best of them quite regularly. Having had the experience, you might want to do yourself the same favor. It will refresh you and keep your life on track.

A kind of "mini-retreat" is possible on a daily basis. It consists in pulling away from your busy schedule for some moments of quiet prayer, eucharist, or scripture reading. Even if these activities do not seem quite as "live" as they were on retreat, they still quietly nourish your relationship with God and hence the influence God will have in your life.

Good News: Jesus said: *"It is not those who say, 'Lord, Lord,' who will enter the kingdom of God, but those who do the will of my Father who is in heaven." (Mt 7:21)*

Jesus' reputation spread more and more, and great crowds gathered to hear him and to be cured of their maladies. He often retired to deserted places and prayed. (Lk 5:15–16)

Christian Action: Listen today for ways God may be speaking to you in what is happening—in the care of a family member or friend, the quiet beauty of nature, the challenge of world events.

WEEK 1: WEDNESDAY

Christian Transformation

In his public ministry, Jesus went about calling people to conversion. "Repent, and believe the good news," was his

6

theme. (Mk 1:15) Repent of what? And what is the good news? New Testament conversion means a change of heart, a whole re-orientation. It becomes clear as one reads the gospel that the change of heart Jesus envisions is not an easy one. It entails a total transformation of our way of looking at things, of valuing, of living life.

One way to map out what it includes is to think of it in terms of relationships. We have four basic relationships as human beings. There is the relationship to God, the relationship to self, the relationship to other people, and the relationship to things. It is in these four areas that Jesus seeks to transform us. When we change the way we relate, we change ourselves, because our self-hood is fashioned by our interaction with the realities around us.

Before we are converted, our four basic relationships tend to look like this. Our relationship to God is non-existent or weak. In relationship to ourself, we either make ourself the center of the world, the only person worth worrying about, or we despise ourself and spend a lot of time beating on ourself internally. In our relationships to others, we tend to care about a few and to have large groups of people whom we either never think about or look down upon and even oppress. As far as our relationship to things is concerned, we tend usually to be acquisitive, hoping to find happiness in the abundance of our possessions.

What happens when, in response to Jesus' summons, we strive to transform our relationships and allow them to be transformed by God's Spirit?

1) *God.* We relate to God in trust. We believe in God as loving and caring, know that we are forgiven and accepted, trust that our life and the life of the world are in good hands. We regard God's values, revealed in Jesus, as the guiding values for our lives.

2) *Self.* We value ourselves, because God values us. We stop listening to internal messages that say, You are stupid, You are worthless, Nobody could care about you. We were made by God, and in us God rejoices, even though we are always imperfect and in process. So we live with security and confidence. But we do not make ourselves the center of the world, because in God's scheme of things we are not the center of the world. Perhaps the best way to image who we are in God's scheme of things is to

image ourselves as co-creators with God, friends who care about God's concerns and exert ourselves to realize God's purposes.

3) *Others.* We see the purpose of life now as learning how to love. And our heart, like the heart of God, becomes as big as the world. We are concerned for all, and, both on the small scale and on the large, we do what we can to see that others have life and have it more abundantly. (Jn 10:10) We are concerned especially for the poor and the rejected, as Jesus was. We do not allow prejudice or fear to separate us from anyone. We discover who people really are by talking with them. And the love we bring them embodies a hope for them which might well go beyond their hope for themselves. It is a hope which empowers, the way Jesus' hope for Zacchaeus empowered Zacchaeus to be much more than he had been. (Lk 19) Legend has it that Diogenes the Greek went about the world with a lantern, looking for a just man. He could not find him. Jesus found him—inside the Good Thief.

4) *Things.* If we take Jesus as model for our way of relating to things, two of his attitudes stand out. The first is his reverence for things, his contemplative stance toward them. Jesus listened to things, and in them he heard the word of God. And so his stories of God are stories of birds, seeds, children, harvests, kings, seasons, weddings, thieves, banquets, sheep, lilies, families. Jesus looked and listened, finding in ordinary reality the parables of God. The other attitude that stands out in him in his relation to things is his detachment. Unlike most people who live in the world, Jesus asked for almost nothing in the way of possessions. It was not in things that he found life, but in God and in people. His exhortation to people was to sell their possessions, give to the poor, and follow him.

When we talk about conversion, or Christian transformation, it is clear now how comprehensive it is. It is not the work of a moment, but the project of a lifetime. The goal is Christlikeness or holiness, which is always partly a gift, partly a choice.

Good News: *"Those things I used to consider gain I have now reappraised as loss in the light of Christ. I have come to rate all as loss in the light of the surpassing knowledge of my Lord Jesus Christ. For his sake I have forfeited everything; I have accounted all else rubbish so that Christ may be my wealth and I may be in him. . . . I wish to know Christ and the power flowing from his resurrection; likewise to know how to share in his sufferings by being formed into the pattern of his death. . . . It is not that I have reached it yet, or have already finished my course; but I am racing to grasp the prize if possible, since I have been grasped by Christ." (Phil 3:7–12)*

Christian Action: Who is there in your family, at work, or at school that you find it especially hard to accept or be around? Spend some time with that person today and see if you can discover him or her in a new way.

WEEK 1: THURSDAY

Difficult People

It seems that each of us finds in our environment a certain number of difficult people with whom we have to live. We wish they were not there, we find it so hard to accept and get along with them. It is bad enough when we have to play on a team, work, or go to school with them. It is worse when the difficult person is a parent, a child, a sibling, a spouse. Is our Christian faith any help in these situations?

Yes, our faith offers us some helpful insights and principles.

1) *The Christian commandment is not to like, but to love, our neighbor.* Liking and loving are quite different things. Liking is having positive *feelings* about others, really enjoying them. Loving is wanting what is good for them, doing what is helpful to them, and not wanting or doing anything to cause harm to them. Sometimes loving is accompanied by no positive feelings at all. One crucial difference between loving and liking is that we have a choice where love is concerned. We can do good to anyone and everyone. We have no such choice about our liking, which, like

9

all our feelings, has a life of its own. That is why the commandment is not about liking.

It is certainly easier when we like the people we must love. But if we find ourselves in the painful situation of not liking a fellow worker or even a parent, child, or sibling, we are not guilty. For feelings are neither good nor bad; they just are. And our freedom of choice remains as to how we will act.

2) *Difficult people are usually unhappy.* We have to look beneath their abrasive behavior to see the dynamic at work. It helps to put ourselves imaginatively into their shoes, and try walking a mile or two. Some staff at a nursing home were having great difficulty putting up with the moodiness, incessant demands, and stubborn opposition of an elderly man who was a resident there. Finally one of them said, "I've been thinking. If I lost my wife, lived in a nursing home, and was confined to a wheelchair with a tube in my nose, I wonder how I would behave."

Not all difficult people have problems of this magnitude. But many of them are genuinely unhappy, have low self-esteem, are lonely, are jealous. And they act out their frustration. When Jesus dealt with people, he looked beneath the surface of their behavior to try to find their hearts. That is why he befriended Zacchaeus and Magdalene, both of whom were despised by others. And by befriending, he changed both of them. As G. K. Chesterton once remarked, the moral of the story "Beauty and the Beast" is that a thing must be loved *before* it is lovable.

3) *Difficult people are a positive opportunity.* They always have something to teach us—about life, about ourselves. They stand as warnings, about pitfalls we could fall into too. Sometimes they show us writ large those small parts of ourselves we deny and try to hide from others. That is precisely why we react so strongly to them.

If we look at the people we dislike, we will often find that we fear them or are jealous of them. If we hang in and deal with them instead of running away, we will learn to be less timid, less thin-skinned, less jealous, less needy of having everyone in our fan club. There is no other way to strengthen our weak muscles except through such wrestling.

4) *It is neither Christian nor good to let other people walk over us.* If difficult people have a right to life, so do we. If they

deserve respect and love, so do we. The commandment is to love our neighbor *as ourselves*. If we allow people to continue to bully us, manipulate us, insult or use us, we do a disservice both to ourselves and to them, and this is a failure in love. When Jesus was slapped in the face by a guard of the high priest, he protested: "If I have said something wrong show me the evidence, but if I spoke the truth why did you hit me?" (Jn 18:23)

We come off retreat with great love toward all humanity and a profound desire for peace. Then we run into our difficult people, and discover again that it is not in the abstract but in the concrete that we must love. In the concrete love is not a sentiment but a challenging practical matter. If we cannot love and live in peace with the individuals we see everyday, how can we as nations possibly ever love and live in peace with each other?

Good News: Love is patient; love is kind. Love is not jealous, it does not put on airs, it is not snobbish. Love is never rude, it is not self-seeking, it is not prone to anger; neither does it brood over injuries. Love does not rejoice in what is wrong but rejoices with the truth. There is no limit to love's forbearance, to its trust, its hope, its power to endure. (1 Cor 13:4–7)

Christian Action: Think about a difficult person in your life. What does this person teach you about yourself? What opportunity for your growth is there in relating to him or her? How might you deal with this person more effectively?

WEEK 1: FRIDAY

Who Needs Me?

I have talked with many people who do not think anybody needs them. They feel completely dispensable. If they died, they are quite sure no one would miss them after the first day.

How can this be? The world is *filled* with needy people. There are children who cry out to be adopted. There are elderly people languishing in nursing homes, longing for someone to talk with. In fact, there are lonely people in every circumstance who badly need someone with whom they can share the joys and struggles of their existence.

There are teenage runaways and street kids. There are poor families who do not have enough to live on. In every city there are soup kitchens in need both of food and of volunteer workers. Men and women in prisons would love a pen pal, a visitor, or almost any kind of workshop or study group.

Organizations working for justice and peace always need volunteers. Political candidates trying to build a more just world always need help in getting elected. Amnesty International is following the cases of prisoners of conscience abroad, trying to save them from torture and death. They organize letter writing campaigns to government leaders. In most major cities a call to the United Way or a similar agency of social concerns would uncover any number of opportunities to help needy people.

The most remarkable trait of Jesus of Nazareth was probably his compassion for suffering people of the sort just described. He felt for the multitudes because they were like sheep without a shepherd. Moved by the suffering of the poor, the sick, and the socially outcast, Jesus welcomed, healed, fed, forgave, encouraged. And he attacked those responsible for the oppression and suffering of so many. He gave no theological explanation of human suffering. Instead, he poured himself into relieving it and asked people to help him.

So, to return to our question: Who needs you? Isn't the question rather: Out of all the people who need you, how many can you help?

But maybe you feel a doubt. Maybe you think you don't have anything to give.

Everybody has something to give, most of us many things. Very few of the forms of assistance named above require any special expertise. Everybody can always give what people need most of all: love. Love translates into time, service, and the sharing of oneself.

The whole idea may sound like work. It is. But there is a

paradox in it. This kind of work is also the way to happiness. The whole meaning of our lives is bound up with love: we find happiness in loving others and being loved in return.

I have seen many people in counseling who have begun by telling me their lives are meaningless. When I start asking questions, I always find these people isolated, cut off from relationships. They say no one needs them. *Naturally* their lives are meaningless and they are miserable if they have no real exchange with others. They say, "I wish someone would love me. How wonderful it would be if I knew someone who would really be concerned about me." They have been sitting for years, waiting for that person to come along. They are angry at their parents, their spouses, their friends, because no one has done this for them.

The way out of this prison is shown in Jesus' simple advice: "Give, and it will be given to you." (Lk 6:38) Extending ourselves for others offers us our best chance of getting what we long for. The cry of the unhappy heart "Will somebody please love me?" is the wrong cry. "Who needs me?" is the question that leads to life.

Good News: Jesus continued his tour of all the towns and villages. He taught in their synagogues, he proclaimed the good news of God's reign, and he cured every sickness and disease. At the sight of the crowds, his heart was moved with pity. They were lying prostrate from exhaustion, like sheep without a shepherd. He said to his disciples: "The harvest is good but laborers are scarce. Beg the harvest master to send out laborers to gather his harvest." (Mt 9:35–38)

Christian Action: Reach out with love today to someone who needs you.

Friendship

There is probably nothing in life we value more than we do our friends. Older people and those near death have often said the greatest satisfaction of their lives has been their friendships. What does friendship have to do with Christian living? At least three connections come to mind. It was from our friends, at least in the broad sense, that we received our faith in the first place. They taught it to us and showed us how to live it. Now, as we move through life, it is impossible to grow as persons or to find happiness except in interaction with friends. Since God wants both growth and happiness for us, God is concerned that we have friends. Finally, and perhaps most important of all, God is present in our experience of human friendship. When our friends love us, it is God's love that they embody and express. They are sacraments of God, and reveal God to us.

It may seem strange to call a friend a sacrament. But a sacrament is simply some visible embodiment of the invisible. The invisible is God. The visible embodiment of God might be almost anything—a flower, the wind, water—as every creature expresses something of God. But it is the human being that enjoys privilege of place among all visible embodiments of God. We are made in God's image, Genesis tells us. We can create, as God creates. Even better, we can love, as God loves. But our loving is not mere external imitation, because God dwells in us. God loves through us, and thus we become the visible embodiment of God's loving action.

God is love, and the person who abides in love abides in God, and God in him or her. (1 Jn 4:16)

One of the foundational claims of the Christian religion is that God loves us. All Christians believe that, at least in their heads. But few people feel it. That is because God is invisible and seems quite distant. What brings God's love home to us and makes it real is the love of another human being. Then we feel it and know it.

> No one has ever seen God. Yet if we love one another, God dwells in us, and God's love is brought to completion in us. (1 Jn 4:12)

This is what Jesus was, the visible embodiment of God's love in the world, the sacrament of God's outreach to people. But this is what all the rest of us are too, or at least are called to be. Now we can see human friendship in a whole different light. It is God who gives to me, God who cherishes and appreciates me, God who comforts and challenges me in my friends. And what they are to me, I am to them too, the same sort of sacrament.

When you think about it, it is really not so strange that all our experiences of love are experiences of God. After all, it is love that heals. It is love that encourages us, freeing us to be ourselves. It is love that makes us grow. It is love and love alone that makes life meaningful. It is love we most hunger for. We know how deep and powerful love is. Little wonder that God is at the bottom of this most potent and highly prized reality.

On the basis of what we have been exploring, we can understand why marriage is one of the seven principal sacraments of the Roman Catholic tradition. For marriage is simply the highest instance of human friendship. The two friends who make the marital commitment will be primary embodiments of God's graciousness to one another all their lives. And those of us who see their faithful, caring, forgiving love will see God in visible form.

Our scripture passage today focuses on Jesus as the sacrament of God's love.

Good News: While Jesus was reclining to eat in Levi's house, many tax collectors and those known as sinners joined him and his disciples at dinner. The number of those who followed him was large. When the scribes who belonged to the Pharisee party saw that he was eating with tax collectors and offenders against the law, they complained to his disciples, "Why does he eat with such as these?" Overhearing the remark, Jesus said to them,

"People who are healthy do not need a doctor; sick people do. I have come to call not the self-righteous, but sinners." (Mk 2:15–17)

Christian Action: Meditate gratefully on your friends today and pray for them. And try to let God love them more compassionately, gently, and generously through you.

WEEK 1: SUNDAY

Finding God's Will

To do God's will was the consuming passion of Jesus' life. "My food is to do the will of the One who sent me, to accomplish God's work." (Jn 4:34) "I do always what pleases the One who sent me." (Jn 8:29) Every disciple of Jesus likewise desires to do God's will. But how do we know what God's will for us is? Is it God's will that I go to Mass every day? That I meditate every day? Is it God's will that I serve on this committee? That I continue in my present job? Might it be God's will that I join a religious order?

Some people believe that God actually has a specific will for us with regard to all such questions, and that we must somehow discover what it is in each case. They look for signs and listen for messages, and they believe they get them. But others say they do not get messages and are poor at reading signs. They also wonder if God is really concerned about how we determine each detail of our lives.

If we look at the program Jesus presents to us in the gospels, it seems a general rather than a specific one, a broad set of guidelines for living under the reign of God. He offers no technique about the details for finding God's will. The implication seems to be that God leaves the working out of the specifics to us. Jesus' legacy to us seems to be: (1) a great summary commandment about loving God and others, (2) his own compelling example of a human life actually based on love, and (3) the gift of his animating spirit.

Then how do we go about finding God's will in our daily lives? We pray that our values be the values of Jesus and our spirit the spirit of Jesus. Then we look at the decisions we have to make and use our best judgment. Where we find decisions particularly difficult or filled with long-range implications, we might seek supplementary input from people who love us and who also seem to have the spirit of Jesus. After consulting them, we use our own best judgment and decide.

But how can we be sure that then we are really doing God's will? Perhaps the question is best answered by an analogy, the analogy of genuinely loving parents and their children. Genuinely loving parents do not legislate the details of their children's lives except when they are very small. As the children emerge into adulthood, the parents give them more and more self-determination until the children reach a point where they are entirely on their own. All the parents want for them is that they be good persons, live worthwhile lives, and be happy. They leave it to their children to decide whether they will go to college or not, marry or not, whom they will marry if they do, what sort of work they will do, where they will live, and how they will spend their time.

God loves us with this same sort of reverence for our individual selfhood and freedom and has this same desire for our happiness. God treats us as adults. The broad guidelines for our lives are given us by God in the teaching and example of Jesus. When we live within these, making the best particular choices we can, we are doing God's will.

Good News: A lawyer, in an attempt to trip him up, asked Jesus, "Teacher, which commandment of the law is the greatest?" Jesus said to him: " 'You shall love the Lord your God with your whole heart, with your whole soul, and with all your mind.' This is the greatest and first commandment. The second is like it: 'You shall love your neighbor as yourself.' On these two commandments the whole law is based, and the prophets as well." (Mt 22:35–40)

Jesus said: "I give you a new commandment: Love one another. Such as my love has been for you, so must your love be for each other. This is how all will know you for my disciples: your love for one another." (Jn 13:34)

Christian Action: As you make decisions today, try to keep in mind the example of Jesus' life and love, and let that guide your choices.

Feeling Good About Yourself

Many of us suffer from low self-esteem. We do not feel good about ourselves, and, as a result, withhold ourselves from other people and from activities we might enjoy and do well at. We compare ourselves unfavorably to others, and envy them their good looks, youth and health, friendships, jobs, and personalities.

Low self-esteem usually stems from early childhood deficits and damage. Our parents did not affirm or encourage us enough. Our siblings or childhood associates made fun of us or criticized us, sometimes branding us with nicknames that burned deep. We had little other information to go on and came away with a negative self-image. How can it be healed?

Fortunately, in the course of our lives God almost always supplies us with what we may not have received as small children. Friends come into our lives who do esteem and love us, and they offer us a basis for believing more in ourselves and liking ourselves. They hold up a mirror to us in which we can see our good qualities and our possibilities. Teachers, counselors, relatives, friends are all the instruments of this gracious rebuilding action of God.

But we ourselves have a crucial role to play in the healing process. We have to *hear* and *believe* the affirming and loving things others say to us, otherwise they make absolutely no difference. We can always screen them out, dismiss them as insincere, argue with them as false, and choose to stay focused on the negative. We have an important choice too in the matter of what kind of music we play in our heads when we are alone. Will we let the critical inner voice keep running us down? Or will we put on more pleasant music? After all, we are made happy not by the amount of love we are given, but by the amount of love we allow ourselves to receive.

In the end, we have to give love to ourselves. The love of others can only prepare us for this and support it. A great day dawns in our life when we can say, "I like myself. I am worthwhile. I have good things to share with others." It helps to say such things to ourselves repeatedly, even when we do not feel them. This is how we change the music in our heads and begin to feel differently about ourselves. Once that happens, it does not matter so much whether others understand and approve everything we do or not, for now we are standing on our own two feet.

What is the ultimate basis on which we can affirm ourselves and feel good about ourselves? It is that God made each of us, and saw that we were good. God does not make junk. "Yes," you might say, "but some of God's creatures are more beautiful than others, and I happen to be one of the least beautiful." Here your childhood damage is showing, and you are insisting on it as truth. You do not see yourself as God sees you, or even as many people see you. Think of the flowers. God made many kinds. It makes little sense for the lily to look at the rose and say, "I do not feel good about myself, for I am not a rose." Both the lily and the rose are beautiful, and each finds enjoyment and glorifies God by being itself.

Good News: God looked at everything that was made, and God found it very good. (Gen 1:31)
  Jesus said: "Love your neighbor as yourself." (Mt 22:39)

Christian Action: Take a few moments today to acknowledge some of your special gifts, and thank God for loving you and creating you.

Prayer

When you made your decision to go on retreat, whether you fully realized it or not you were making a decision to let God into your life. This is not an easy decision because, although it is exciting to let God in, it is also scary. The decision about regular prayer is exactly the same. Again the issue is whether to open your life to God or not. Again the feelings are a mixture of desire and fear.

Why do we pray? Probably for the same reason we go on retreat: we feel a need for something. We are lonely for a more faithful companionship than ordinary human association gives. We want a deeper meaning than superficial experience offers. We need help with struggles and problems that seem greater than our resources. We want to feel again a comfort we have known only in the presence of God. Listen to how the Psalms, the bible's book of prayers, express the feelings that move people to prayer.

O God, you are my God whom I seek;
 for you my flesh pines and my soul thirsts
 like the earth, parched, lifeless, and without water. (Ps
  63:2)

Only in God is my soul at rest;
 from God comes my salvation. (Ps 62)

I lift up my eyes to the mountains;
 whence shall help come to me?
 My help is from the Lord, who made heaven
  and earth. (Ps 121)

We do not stay with prayer very long on the basis of a mere "ought." Prayer takes too much time, and is often rather uneventful. We stay with it only on the basis of the sort of need or attraction described above. We stay with it too because we notice that it has a good effect on us. "When I pray, I feel centered as I move through my day," a woman said. "I have an inner strength."

"I wish I knew how to pray," a man said. "You know how to pray," I said, "if you know how to hold a child in your lap, if you know how to embrace your wife, if you know how to be quiet and fish on a lake. Prayer is a natural activity, and everyone knows how to pray who knows how to look, how to love."

There is no "right way" to pray, no one "method." We each pray in our own way, as we each walk in our own way. Some people like to sit in a church or chapel and just be when they pray. Some like to take a walk. Some do yoga, take up the lotus position, and focus on their breathing or on a candle flame. Some take up the guitar and sing. Others dance before the Lord. Some open scripture and slowly read. Some relive experiences which are still in their awareness because they were either especially painful or especially joyous, and ponder the meaning of these experiences with God. Some use their imaginations and encounter God in various symbols.

What do all these approaches have in common? All of them are some kind of relating, an I-Thou, a being together, a mutual awareness and influence. All of them are some kind of listening and responding, even if that give-and-take is as quiet and implicit as when an old married couple read the newspaper before the same fire.

"But I always have distractions when I pray," a boy said, "and I just can't get rid of them." Yes, but your communion with God is taking place at a deeper level. That bonding is not a matter of the mind, which is where your distractions are. "Let the fool run in the palace," St. Teresa said of distractions. "Don't worry about him." Just keep coming back to the quiet presence. If a certain distraction continues to intrude, you might stop fighting it and make it instead the focus of your prayer. It could be reminding you of the most important thing going on in your life right now. Bring it into the dialogue with God. In any case, do not be discouraged by distractions. You have made the decision to let God into your life, and so God is there. The rest is secondary.

Good News: Immediately afterward he insisted that his disciples get into the boat and precede him to the other side toward Bethsaida, while he dismissed the crowd. When he had taken leave of them, he went off to the mountain to pray. (Mk 6:45)

Christian Action: Take some time to pray today. Do it in whatever way seems most natural to you.

WEEK 2: WEDNESDAY

Loneliness

Loneliness is a familiar experience to most people. Little children often feel it, though they do not know its name. Older people who have lost their life-companions know it intimately. So do many people in between, including the married. Is it a permanent condition that cannot be helped, or a problem that can be solved? When it is present, what does it mean?

Our loneliness has much in common with our sexuality. Both are signs of our incompleteness and of our profound yearning for companionship and closeness. So both speak of God's purpose for us, deeply embedded in the way we are made. Just as hunger tells us we need food, the pain of loneliness forces us to think about the companionship we need, and so points us in the direction of the solution. When we feel loneliness we can rightly interpret: God has made me to be with others, and this inner emptiness and pain I feel is a sign that I must reach out more. With whom can I share myself? And who needs to share with me?

For everybody is in the same situation, made the same way, feeling the same need. Some people are even lonelier than you, though their exterior may not show it. They may look "cool," apparently all set. But often it is just a cover, their way of putting on a less vulnerable face. Other people look positively unfriendly, even hostile. They seem to carry a sign that says: Do not approach.

Others look very busy, fussing with things, talking either to themselves or to anyone within earshot about whatever it is they are busy about. You have probably used all or some of these coping devices yourself, and so can see through them. An older woman once remarked very perceptively, "You can safely presume that other persons are lonely. If you greet them and show a little interest, they will warm up to you. It doesn't matter what they look like to start with."

Loneliness has another meaning besides signaling our call to involvement with other people. It indicates a deeper need too, our need for God. "You have made us for yourself, O Lord," St. Augustine says, "and our hearts are restless until they rest in you." Sometimes our loneliness is a call to prayer. On the eve of his passion, when his companions fell asleep in the garden, Jesus turned to God. The Roman Catholic theologian, Karl Rahner, invites us to brave our own loneliness sometimes, and, instead of looking for other solutions, to go down into the dark cavern of our inner space and seek the quiet, benevolent Presence that is there.

In talking with people who enjoy a strong bond with God, I have frequently found that they had very lonely childhoods. In the absence of any significant human companionship, they developed a friendship with God, the only one who was around. What seemed a curse at the time, childhood loneliness, has become a great blessing in their lives, as the friendship they developed with God has grown through the years.

Is loneliness, then, a permanent part of the human condition in this world or a problem that can be solved? It seems to be both. Its meaning is clear: We find our fulfillment only in sharing life with others, and ultimately in sharing life with God. The pain of loneliness is a prod in those directions, a prod we need because relationships are risky and sometimes we back away from them.

Good News:

> *You, O Lord, are my shepherd; I shall not want.*
> *In verdant pastures you give me repose;*
> *Beside restful waters you lead me;*
>   *you refresh my soul.*

24

You guide me in right paths for your name's sake.
Even though I walk in the dark valley
I fear no evil, for you are at my side;
With your rod and your staff you give me courage.

You spread the table before me
in the sight of my foes;
You anoint my head with oil;
my cup overflows
Only goodness and kindness follow me
all the days of my life;
And I shall dwell in your house, O Lord,
for years to come. (Ps 23)

Christian Action: Make an effort today to talk to someone you see who is lonely, even though they may be masking that loneliness with an exterior that puts you off.

WEEK 2: THURSDAY

Loving People Who Are Different

When we grasp the idea that love is the center of the Christian life, we usually reflect on our close relationships and work on improving them. This is good. There is another area we need to examine too if we want to love as Jesus did. How far does our love extend? Jesus' love was as large as humanity. In the lives of most of us, prejudice, recognized and unrecognized, sharply limits the scope of our love.

Some of us do not like blacks. Others do not like whites. Some do not like women. Others do not like men. Some of us hate gays. Others hate communists. Some hate Jews. Some cannot stand liberals. Others despise conservatives. Some look down on

Roman Catholics. Others scorn Mormons. Some of us hate every kind but our own, and we do not like too many of them. So we just take good care of our families and steer clear of everybody else. Usually, with this kind of love, things do not go too well in our families either.

Where does prejudice come from? Well, the word means "prejudgment." A prejudice is not a conclusion drawn from experience. It is a judgment made without the benefit of experience. We usually inherit our prejudices from others and do not bother checking to see whether their judgments are true. Once in a while, our prejudice is based on a personal experience, but often on just a single instance. From that one experience, we stereotype a whole group and resolve to have nothing more to do with them. Prejudice is rooted in laziness, ignorance, and fear.

A woman told me, "I prejudged and hated all gay people. Then one day my son got up the courage to tell me he was gay. I cried. He cried. In the weeks that followed I started really listening to him, and I learned so much. Gradually he brought some of his friends over. I came to see that gay people are wonderful human beings who carry a deep suffering. I really had my eyes opened. Now my son and I are the best of friends."

Our prejudices are often rooted in our own feelings of inadequacy. We fear gays because we fear the part of ourselves that is gay. We fear the opposite sex because we feel weak in the areas in which they are typically strong, or because we feel weak in the areas in which *our* sex is supposed to be strong. Sometimes we look around for *any* group of people we can feel superior to because deep down we feel inferior to almost everybody. The possibility of a broader love of humankind begins in the difficult act of self-love.

The story of the woman with the gay son shows the other important part of the cure for our prejudices. If prejudice is rooted in laziness, ignorance, and fear, we must summon up the courage to initiate some direct contact, some real dialogue, with whatever kind of person it is we have prejudged and rejected. Mere acquaintance ("Oh, yeah, I've worked with a lot of 'em") is not enough. We really have to listen, trying to understand. We have to ask questions, suspending judgment for a long time. Gradually understanding comes, and with it empathy. Now we are on a completely different footing with the person. We have come in touch with their humanity.

A man can beat a woman only if he forgets that she is a person. A soldier can apply instruments of torture to a captive only if he has depersonalized him or her. A state can execute a criminal only if it sets aside the fact that he is a human being. A nation can fire a nuclear weapon at another nation only if it blots out the truth that that nation is composed of families like our own. How wary we must be of our labels and stereotypes, how alert to our blindness and irrational fears.

Jesus saw the heart. There were prejudices in his society too, against women, tax collectors, prostitutes, lepers, Samaritans, non-Jews. These were the very people Jesus reached out to, got best acquainted with, and came to love the most.

Good News: To you who hear me I say: Love your enemies, do good to those who hate you; bless those who curse you, and pray for those who maltreat you. . . . If you love those who love you, what credit is that to you? Even sinners love those who love them. . . . Be compassionate as your Father is compassionate. Do not judge, and you will not be judged. Do not condemn, and you will not be condemned. Pardon, and you shall be pardoned. Give, and it shall be given to you. Good measure pressed down, shaken together, running over, will they pour into your lap. For the measure you measure with will be measured back to you. (Lk 6:27–38)

Christian Action: Start praying for those people you tend to write off or hate. This will help you to see them as human persons like yourself. Then try some of that direct contact described above.

WEEK 2: FRIDAY

Religious Feelings, Religious Living

One of the most common mistakes we make as religious people is to confuse feeling with reality. We think that if we feel close to God and talk religiously, we are holy. If we do not feel anything, we are convinced we are far from God and something is wrong. So we begin to think we are holy on retreat, and are sure we have "lost it" not long after we are returned to our ordinary routine.

Yet Jesus said, "It is by their fruits that you will know them." (Mt 7:20) And also: "Not everyone who cries out, 'Lord, Lord,' will enter the kingdom of God, but those who do the will of my Father in heaven." (Mt 7:21) What we need to learn to attend to is our behavior, not our feelings. For the cardinal truth is this: we can always do the good, even in the absence of good feelings. And we can neglect to do what cries out to be done all the while we are filled with holy feelings.

There is no question about the fact that feeling the presence and love of God is a wonderful experience, and that it nourishes our faith life by convincing us of the truth. The good life is much easier when we are supported by a sense of the Presence. But every spiritual veteran knows that feelings of this kind are notoriously unreliable. We cannot produce them, and we cannot sustain them. There is but one thing under our control, and it is the important thing. It is the power of choice about how we will live.

As persons touched by the love of God, we want to grow in our faith, our hope, our love. But what is true faith? Is it true faith to believe when our feelings of God's love are so strong that there can be no doubt? Or is it true faith to believe when there is absolutely no sign? Is it true hope to trust when we can see that God is at work and everything is coming out beautifully? Or is it true hope to trust when there is no palpable assurance at all? Is it true love to give when one receives even more in return? Or is it true love to give when nothing at all comes back? Could it be that God withdraws that clear presence and those warm feelings precisely so that our faith, our hope, and our love might become more genuine?

One of the little known facts of the lives of the saints is that they frequently went for years without any feelings of God's presence or love. It practically killed them, as their whole lives were oriented to God and taken up with God. As their thirst went unquenched and their prayer continued unanswered, they felt they had been abandoned altogether, and that it was probably because of their sins. All the while, those who knew them best experienced a clear presence of God in them and a marked influence of God on their behavior. But they could not feel any of it. They had to live by faith.

The experience of the Christian life as it goes much of the time is well symbolized in that scene where the disciples are out in a boat alone on a stormy lake. The winds are howling and the waves are coming over the side, and the one who got them into this is nowhere to be found. He was last seen on a mountain some time ago. (Mk 6:45) But that is only scene one. In scene two Jesus comes back to them, in the darkness of the night, walking on the water. And he chides them for their lack of faith.

Good News: Who is the faithful, far-sighted servant whom the master has put in charge of his household to dispense food at need? Happy that servant whom his master discovers at work on his return! I assure you, he will put him in charge of all his property. (Mt 24:45–47)

Christian Action: Read a biography of a Christian saint you have found attractive.

WEEK 2: SATURDAY

Sin

Sin is not something we usually like to think about. Yet it is a reality in our lives. If we are serious about the Christian life, we need to have some fairly clear conceptions of what sin is and how it works in our lives. The question is not an easy one. What is sin really? Is masturbation a sin? Is a sarcastic remark a sin? Is it a sin to miss Mass on Sunday? Is being angry a sin?

Many people were brought up to think sin is breaking a commandment. There are many laws and rules. When an action goes against one of them, it is a sin. God keeps a record. There are big sins (mortal) and little sins (venial). If you keep all the laws and rules, there is no sin in your life.

That is the legalistic approach to sin. A different approach, one that is closer to the biblical understanding, is being recovered in Christian teaching today. In the bible sin is always viewed within the context of a love relationship between God and ourselves. Sin is the failure to live the implications of that relatedness. God loves us and has a purpose for our lives. That purpose is that we grow into the fullness of human personhood. To be fully human is above all to be loving. God has a purpose for the whole world too, that humankind be united in bonds of love, so that *everyone* in the world might have life and reach the fullness of his or her personhood. We live always in relationship with God and within that loving purpose. When we fail to cooperate with it, acting instead against it, we sin.

Fundamentally, then, sin is always a refusal to love. It is a frustration of God's loving purpose for me and for the world. It is not primarily the breaking of a law, but the injuring of an interpersonal relationship between myself and God and myself and other people. In sin, someone—myself or someone else—always gets hurt, is hindered, is violated. This happens because I prefer some immediate gratification to my own real good and the good of others. Now it is because persons whom God genuinely loves are hurt—myself and others—that God is grieved by human sinning. This reality is scarcely expressed by speaking of an "offended divine majesty."

Because of our profound interpersonal relationship with God in love, the biblical prophets called all human sinning adultery. In so expressing themselves, they were not talking about our sleeping with married people's spouses. They were thinking about our marriage with God, which they called covenant, a sacred bondedness in mutual love. To be unfaithful to that in any manner was adulterous. Jesus meant this same thing when he called the people of his day "a wicked and adulterous generation."

The contemporary theology of sin locates sin more in tendencies, patterns, and habits than in particular acts. Many theologians therefore suggest talking about sinfulness rather than sins. We have tendencies, for instance, toward dishonesty, toward prejudice, toward using other people, toward thinking only of ourselves. These tendencies show up in the patterns and habits of our daily lives, and we are often scarcely aware of them. Then something happens that brings us face to face with one of them, and we realize what we have been doing. We have just been confronted with our sinfulness. Now we have a choice, to break with the pattern or to continue it.

This suggests a different way of confessing our sins, whether we confess them to the person we have hurt or to a priest in the sacrament of reconciliation. Instead of saying, "I was uncharitable five times," I might say, "Lately I've been very preoccupied with my own concerns, and I have not been present to my family, really listened to them, or been at all alert to what they need." Or I might go to my spouse or best friend and say, "I think I've hurt you lately by being cold and distant, and I am sorry. I've come to realize that at the bottom of that there is a resentment I'm feeling, and I want to talk with you about it."

Basic to our understanding of sin is remembering that we have a covenant of love with God, and that true life is God's purpose for us and everyone else. What sin breeds is death. So we keep an eye on the patterns of behavior in our lives, to see whether life-giving love is really being expressed in them. Where we see the opposite of love, we work to change the pattern. In all of this we must learn to be patient with ourselves. God is patient with us. Learning to love well takes a lifetime.

Good News: Because you are God's chosen ones, holy and beloved, clothe yourselves with heartfelt mercy, with kindness, humility, meekness, and patience. Bear with one another; forgive whatever grievances you have against one another. Forgive as the Lord has forgiven you. Over all these virtues put on love, which binds the rest together and makes them perfect. Christ's peace must reign in your hearts, since as members of the one body you have been called to that peace. (Col 3:12–15)

Christian Action: Go and be reconciled today, or as soon as you can, with someone you have been hurting by the pattern of your actions. Decide on at least one way to begin changing the pattern.

WEEK 2: SUNDAY

Images of God

How shall we describe God? We *experience* God, but, as the fourth gospel puts it, "No one has ever *seen* God." (Jn 1:18) Nor can our minds understand God, for God is a great mystery. The Hebrew people experienced God long before we did, and the way they dealt with the problem of description was to use images and stories to try to get across what they had encountered.

Jesus, a Hebrew, did the same thing. It was through many stories of God that he tried to convey to us who God is, what God is doing, and what God wants. We call these stories parables. Jesus employed images too. His favorite image for God was Father. The Hebrews had not used that image very much at all. In fact Jesus went further in trying to depict God's gentle, familiar love. He called God "Abba," the name Hebrew children called their fathers. The word means "daddy" or "papa."

What we have sometimes forgotten is that these images of God are just that: images. That includes Jesus' favorite image, Father. We have sometimes mistaken these images for the mystery itself. So most Christians speak of God as "he" and "him," as if God were really masculine. This has unfortunate effects. One is to reinforce the sexism of the culture, implicitly to validate male dominance. Another is to limit the ways in which we can experience God. People who have had mostly painful experiences with their human fathers, for example, have great difficulty relating with any warmth or confidence to a God presented in exclusively fatherly terms.

To guard against this difficulty, the God of the Hebrews gave them a commandment: Make no graven image. And so we have no art depicting the God of the Hebrews. Once there is an image, it is so easy to confuse the image with the reality. When the Hebrews asked God for a name they could use, God's reply was, "I am." (Ex 3:14) It is pretty hard to draw a picture of that.

With a profound sense of the incomprehensible mystery, the Hebrews used masculine, feminine, and impersonal images for God in the bible. God is King, Warrior, Judge. God is a woman giving birth, a woman suckling her infant at the breast, lady wisdom seeking people in the streets and inviting them to dinner. God is light, thunder, an eagle, water, bread. One of Jesus' images of God is that of a woman tirelessly sweeping the house for her lost coin, searching for money that is terribly important to her. An image Jesus uses for himself is that of a hen wanting to gather her chicks under her wings.

This rich multiplicity of biblical images keeps us aware of the many facets of the mystery of God. The various images also open us to different ways of relating to God. We have fallen into idolatry as a church, taking our male image of God for the reality. We have suffered the impoverishment of our social and individual spiritual lives as a consequence. The great Christian mystics, both men and women, have used the feminine and impersonal images of God as well as the masculine in their prayer and spiritual writings. To recontact this tradition is to experience a wonderful liberation. This is true not just for women, but for men as well.

So as you pray, or as you walk through your day, you might try imaging God in feminine or in impersonal ways. How do you feel relating to God as mother? What insights and feelings are yours when you think of God as light suffusing all things, as creative energy deep down in reality, as healing power quietly at work in the world's brokenness? This or some other reimaging might be the key that unlocks the power of your own relationship with God.

Good News: Jesus said, *"What woman, if she has ten silver pieces and loses one, does not light a lamp and sweep the house in a diligent search until she has retrieved what she lost? And when she finds it, she calls in her friends and neighbors to say, 'Rejoice with me! I have found the silver piece I lost.' I tell you, there will be* the same kind of joy before the angels of God over one repentant sinner.'' (Lk 15:8–10)

Christian Action: Experiment with feminine and impersonal images of God in your prayer and daily life. See what effect they have on you. Use the images that open you to the mystery of God.

WEEK 3: MONDAY

Feeling Angry

Is it a sin to be angry? Is it possible to love someone and also be angry with him or her?

If it were a sin to be angry, Jesus would be guilty of it. He took up a whip one day and drove the buyers and sellers out of the temple, overturning their tables. Another day he addressed the Jewish leadership in these terms: "Woe to you scribes and Pharisees, hypocrites! You travel over sea and land to make a single convert, but once he is converted you make a devil of him twice as wicked as yourselves!" (Mt 23:15) These are not the words or deeds of a man in an affable mood. Clearly Jesus was angry.

Anger is not a bad thing in itself. It is a normal and useful human emotion. We have no more control over whether anger will arise than we do over whether sexual feelings will arise. Both are instinctive and prior to any free choice. Every animal, including the human, is equipped with anger as an immediate response to certain stimuli. Anger is a warning that the organism's well-being is threatened. It prepares the animal for fight or flight. The human animal has the additional option of peaceful negotiation. So the moral question is not whether we will *feel* anger but what we will *do* with our anger. Will we use it to destroy or to build?

Anger arises even in the closest human relationships. It is quite compatible with love, which endures at a deeper level. Anger has to do with particular problems that need addressing, and love demands that they be addressed. If two people cannot deal honestly with the anger that arises inevitably in close relating, they cannot enjoy real intimacy either. They may be able to keep everything smooth on the surface by holding anger in, but emo-

35

tionally each has moved to a safe distance. Far more intimate are those friends who clash once in a while, work the problem through, and end up embracing.

Anger is probably the most difficult emotion for most of us to deal with. It is very hard to listen to someone who is angry with us. But it is also difficult for many of us to express our own anger. First, we may think it is wrong to feel this way. Then we hesitate to express it either because we do not want to hurt the other person's feelings or because we fear it will make the other person dislike us. But when we hold anger in, we find that it takes a heavy toll on our psyches and even on our bodies.

In working anger through with someone, it is helpful to realize that the anger is a secondary, not a primary, emotion. There is always another feeling beneath it: hurt, frustration, or fear. For example, when people's questions threaten us, we often react angrily. When people hurt us by slighting or insulting us, anger arises immediately. If we can share the fear or the hurt with the other person, it is easier for that person to hear and understand us than it is if we just take out our anger on them. So too when someone comes at us angrily, it makes it easier to bear if we can remember that under this harsh exterior there lie some rather tender human feelings: hurt, frustration, or fear. If we can address *these* feelings, and apologize for somehow causing them, the other person will feel understood and the anger will drain away.

Let us pray for the spirit of Jesus, that we might learn how to understand and deal with anger in more constructive ways.

Good News: On the last and greatest day of the festival, Jesus stood up and cried out: "If anyone thirsts, let them come to me; let them drink who believe in me. Scripture has it: 'From within him rivers of living water shall flow.' " Here he was referring to the Spirit, whom those that came to believe in him were to receive. There was, of course, no Spirit as yet, since Jesus had not yet been glorified. (Jn 7:37-39)

Christian Action: Reflect on some times when you have been angry. (1) Can you distinguish between the feeling of anger, which arises spontaneously, and the point where your free choices about it begin? (2) Can you name the feeling which lies under the anger? (3) Can you remember times when you have used anger constructively and achieved a closer relationship through it?

WEEK 3: TUESDAY

Working Anger Through

Many of us fear anger, our own and others', because we have seen its potential for harm. Anger *can* indeed be destructive. Given free reign, it can inflict deep emotional wounds, physical injury, even murder. Are there ways we as Christians can deal more constructively with anger? Here are some suggestions.

1) *Report anger, don't vent it.* That means simply to state it, tell the person about it. "I'm feeling angry at you because you were late." Reporting is different from venting. We vent anger when we hit, throw things, or rant and rave. We vent anger in a subtler way when we withdraw and punish by silence. Venting is not constructive; reporting is. Sometimes we need a cooling-off period before we can report without venting.

2) *Tie your anger to concrete outward behavior.* Avoid vague generalizations, e.g., "You never pay any attention to me," and the imputing of motives, "You said that to upset me." We are never sure of what another person's motives or feelings are, and others resent our trying to read their minds. Anything that sounds like an accusation will put them on the defensive. It is better just to describe the outwardly observable actions which provoked the anger. "It really bothered me how much you kept to yourself all evening when we were with my family." That is a feeling tied to a behavior. It is information for the other person. Now it is the other person's turn to speak.

3) *Assume joint responsibility for the anger, and work it through together.* This requires a previous agreement. For that matter, all four of these points might well be the substance of an explicit agreement between two friends or spouses who want to

deal more constructively with their anger. The present point is that if I am angry with you, that does not necessarily mean you have done something wrong. The problem may lie with me: in my unreasonable expectations or my interpretation of what happened. It could, of course, be a failing on your part. Or it could be some combination of the two. We will not know until we talk it through. Talking it through with real openness to the truth is hard. We both have to be willing to listen and to look at the matter from each other's point of view. We may be called upon to change our attitude or our behavior or both if love is not being served by what we are doing. This is why the whole matter of conflict between persons is a central concern of Christian spirituality. There is often a call to personal growth in it.

4) *Don't let anger build to the boiling point.* Work with it while it is still manageable. It is when we hold anger in until it explodes that it is difficult to deal with constructively.

It goes without saying that we have neither the time nor the energy to work through anger every time we feel it. We have to decide whether it is worth it. That depends on the importance of the issue and the importance of the relationship. There is a certain amount of vexation in life that it is probably wiser just to write off.

If we find ourselves angry a lot—easily irritated, and having angry conversations in our heads with many people—we need to look at the underlying cause. It may be some deep hurt we have suffered, some painful memory that keeps getting scratched and needs to be dealt with directly. It can also be a sign that we are not taking good care of ourselves—getting enough sleep, having enough fun, getting our needs for love met. We might also have the bad habit of nursing grudges. We can make or keep ourselves angry by the sorts of scenes we focus on in our heads. We can keep rehearsing some unhappy incident, interpreting it again in the worst way, making more vicious responses than we were able to think of at the time, and so fanning the flames of anger. Or we can choose to set it aside and move on to more pleasant topics. Finding ourselves angry too much concerns us as Christians, because it is impossible for a chronically angry person to love very much.

One way to bring some sort of closure to anger we cannot

express to the person who has hurt us, whether because the person has died or is someone who would not listen, is to write a letter to the person, a letter we will not send. In it we express all the anger we feel, just to get it out of our system. We might also imagine the person sitting in an empty chair across from us, and express all our anger out loud. Having gotten it out in one of these two ways, we let go of it, surrendering it to God and asking for the grace to forgive.

Good News: *Your love must be sincere. Detest what is evil, cling to what is good. Love one another with the affection of sisters and brothers. Anticipate each other in showing respect. Do not grow slack, but be fervent in spirit; it is the Lord you serve. Rejoice in hope, be patient in trial, persevere in prayer.... Do not be wise in your own estimation. Never repay injury with injury. See that your conduct is honorable in the eyes of all. If possible, live peaceably with everyone.... Do not be conquered by evil but conquer evil with good. (Rm 12:9–18)*

Christian Action: Prayerfully become aware of ways in which anger may be blocking your ability to love in an important relationship. Then use the steps above to work through the anger you are feeling towards that person.

WEEK 3: WEDNESDAY

Christian Joy

Retreat is usually a time of deep joy. But what about daily life in the world? The Bible says that Christians should be joyful, but how can anybody possibly be joyful when life is so difficult? To live is to struggle with work, with relationships, with sexuality, with loneliness, with other painful feelings. To live is to be met with disappointments, frustrations, failures, sickness, accidents, losses. Joy in today's world is even harder. The daily news is filled with stories of disaster, corruption, and massive human suffering. How can anyone with any awareness be joyful?

Against all the odds, Christian joy is possible because:

1) *Jesus reveals God as gracious and kind.* This allows us to live in peace with our own guilt, our failures, our imperfections. God does not judge us harshly, is not quick to condemn. God is rather like a gracious friend who gives us the time and space we need to grow, who is patient and understanding, who does not expect us to get it right the first time. God has not rejected us even if we have rejected ourselves.

2) *For those who love God, God makes everything work together for good.* (Rom 8:28) This statement of Paul's sums up a whole theology of hope. God is at work in everything trying to bring some good out of it—even out of the tragedies that befall us, even out of our own and other people's sins. In the Christian vision, nothing is simply waste or loss. Even the worst experiences contain blessings, if we take the trouble to seek God's activity within them. Christian joy then is based on a certain confidence that faith gives. "God brings the dead to life and calls into being the things that are not," Paul says. (Rom 4:17) The clearest revelation of this hidden but powerful activity of God is in the tragic death of Jesus, which God transforms into life and salvation for Jesus and everyone else.

3) *God can take care of the world.* God was taking care of it long before we came along, and will be long after we are gone. Our worrying about the world does not do it any good, nor can any of us by our poor powers greatly affect it. Let us do what we can, but then let us give it back to God and relax more. Then joy could begin to have a space to grow. Trust in God is an essential condition for joy. Becoming like a little child is key to it.

In sum, if we don't have to worry so much about our failings, if we can trust that even in our worst experiences God is at work with us to bring good out of them, and if we can believe that God really loves and cares for all the people in this world, perhaps we can set our hearts more at ease. We will not necessarily be happy-go-lucky, but we can be at peace, even quietly joyful deep inside ourselves. And if we want our joy to grow, we will keep trying to live as Jesus did. "All this I tell you that my joy may be yours and your joy may be complete." (Jn 15:11)

Good News: Jesus said: "I have told you these things so that in me you might have peace. In the world you will have distress; but have confidence, for I have overcome the world." (Jn 16:33)
"Come to me, all you who labor and are heavily burdened, and I will give you rest. Take my yoke upon you and learn from me, for I am meek and humble of heart, and you will find rest for your souls. For my yoke is easy, and my burden is light." (Mt 11:28-30)

Christian Action: Reflect on the times when you become downhearted and lose your joy. What is usually at the root of the problem? Make it a habit to say the "serenity prayer" of St. Teresa:

> "God, give me the serenity to accept the things I cannot change,
> the courage to change the things I can,
> and the wisdom to know the difference."

WEEK 3: THURSDAY

The Cross of Jesus

Christians sometimes talk as if love of the cross were the centerpiece of Jesus' teaching and Christianity's highest ideal.

The fact is, Jesus never taught love of the cross. He never said, "The harder thing is the better thing," "Seek suffering," or "Beware of joy." Nowhere in the gospels does Jesus say to a sick, hungry, or grieving person: "This is good for you," "This is God's will for you," or "This is a special mark of God's love for you." What Jesus did was spend himself relieving human suf-

41

fering, and he invited others to help him. This strongly suggests that he regarded suffering as an evil.

Yet Jesus did say, "If you want to come after me, you must deny yourself, take up your cross, and follow in my steps." (Mk 8:34) What does this mean? What is this "cross" which followers of Jesus are supposed to take up?

Judging from Jesus' total statement, taking up the cross is something that we *choose* to do, not something that happens to us, and it is an action we do in a context, a context of *following Jesus*. In the gospels, following Jesus means being with him and doing what he did. What did he do? And where does the cross fit into his life?

Jesus spent himself for other people. He labored to make life better for them. He was especially concerned about the poor and marginal members of the human community, and in espousing their cause he came into conflict with the rich and powerful. He became a nuisance to the people who were benefiting from the system, "the establishment," and they got rid of him. The same thing has happened to many other people, before Jesus and since. What is notable about Jesus' life is not that he sought suffering, which he did not, but that he was driven entirely by love. He denied himself (his own interest) and sought the welfare of others. This is costly, both in the labor itself and often in the consequence of such labor. The cross, then, is the symbol of Jesus' love, of his willingness to give his life for others. It is to take up this same burden of spending oneself in love for others that he calls all who wish to follow him. Now we can understand more clearly how taking up the cross is a *choice,* and that we do it in the context of *following Jesus.*

There is a whole other category of sufferings that Christians and all other persons face in life as part of the human condition— sickness, failure, wrongs inflicted by others, etc. Jesus' call to us here is not to embrace and love these things, but to *struggle against* them as he himself did in God's name. For these are not God's will at all. Poverty is not God's will. Unemployment is not God's will, and neither is failure. Crippling injuries are not God's will, and neither is disease. The social injustices that oppress people are not God's will, but, like so many of the other evils named here, are the result of human sinfulness. If we have a nuclear war, let us not say it was God's will, since God so clearly stands against everything that a nuclear war entails. The adage "Everything happens for a reason" is misleading insofar as it suggests that everything that happens is planned by God. A more adequate way to state our faith vision is, "In everything that happens, even the worst tragedies, God works with us to bring some good."

So what should be the Christian attitude and response to these latter sufferings we have been enumerating? Our first response should be to struggle against and overcome them if possible, because they are not good but evil. Our second response comes only after the first, and it is to accept what we cannot overcome, and to do so in hope. Our hope is rooted in the goodness and power of God, who, we trust, can bring some good out of it somehow if we are open to it.

We need that hope because we live with considerable suffering even after all our best efforts. It is helpful to know that God did not inflict this suffering on us, that, in fact, it may be exactly the opposite of what God really wanted for us, and that God grieves with us in our suffering as any friend would. It is consoling to know that God is at work with us, in the hidden depths of our suffering, to help us bring some good out of it.

What good? Our own experience tells us. It may be more evident if we look at past sufferings rather than present ones, because we can see the past in clearer perspective. Suffering makes us patient and strong. Suffering mellows us. Suffering teaches us compassion for the pain and struggle of others, and so increases our capacity for love. Suffering deepens our faith and our trust in God. Suffering gives us a more profound knowledge of ourselves. Suffering opens us to the experience of being loved by others. Suffering makes us humbler. We often see in people who have suffered much a fuller range of the best human qualities than we see in those who have had an easier time. But it is not necessarily so. Suffering can harden and embitter us too. It all depends on the spirit in which we live through it.

Good News:

> *Jesus stood up in the synagogue and said:*
> *The spirit of the Lord has been given to me,*

for the Lord has anointed me.
The Lord has sent me to bring good news to the poor,
to proclaim liberty to captives
and to the blind new sight,
to set the downtrodden free,
to proclaim the Lord's year of favor. (cf. Is 61:1-2)
    . . . This text is being fulfilled today even as you listen.
    (Lk 4:18-21)

Christian Action: Spend some time in prayerful reflection today on Jesus' call to you, "Take up your cross and follow me." What does that ask of you? Try to bring at least one concrete action out of it.

WEEK 3: FRIDAY

Forgiveness

One of our deepest struggles is the struggle to forgive. When we have been deeply hurt, or suffered a serious loss through the inconsiderate or malicious action of someone else, we find it very hard to put it behind us and be reconciled with that person. Sometimes it is a particular action that leaves us feeling hurt and angry. Sometimes it is a pattern of action. Many people find it hard to forgive their parents for the whole way they raised them, or a former friend or spouse for all the pain he or she caused.

Yet forgiveness is a main theme in the teaching of Jesus. "Be merciful as your heavenly Father is merciful," he says. (Lk 6:36) And when Peter asks how often he has to forgive the same offense, Jesus answers "seventy times seven times." (Mt 18:22) Jesus' lived example of forgiveness also stands out, especially his forgiveness from the cross.

How can we better manage this difficult part of loving? There is no way to make it easy, but perhaps the following ideas can help.

1) *We need to ask God's assistance.* Forgiveness sometimes

feels impossible. We have to ask God repeatedly to do for us what we cannot do for ourselves, to take away our heart of stone and give us a heart of flesh.

2) *We are sinners too.* We have hurt other people. If we can accept ourselves as persons who are sometimes selfish, inconsiderate, even mean, as caught up in the broken human condition along with everyone else, it helps us accept other people with their sinfulness too.

3) *Seeing the persons who hurt us in their own context puts matters in a new light.* What was their background? What was going on in their lives when the offense happened? Usually if we can lift ourselves out of our own situation and imagine ourselves in other people's shoes, we can more easily understand why they did what they did. And when we understand, it is easier to forgive. Often, we learn, people did to us what was done to them, or failed to do for us what no one ever did for them. Sometimes too we can see that it was not malice that motivated them, but sheer preoccupation with the struggles of their own lives.

4) *Forgiveness is much easier if the other person apologizes.* It is hardest when the other person does not seem to be aware of any wrongdoing. Sometimes the only way others will be brought to see and acknowledge wrongdoing is if we go and tell them. This is hard to do, of course, but it is sometimes crucial to being able to finish the matter off and gain peace of mind.

5) *Forgiveness is not always the proper response.* Some patterns of action are ongoing and are simply not acceptable. Take wife-beating, for example. A woman has to insist on change in a case like this, or remove herself from the situation. Even in matters less severe, it may be more a question of talking with the offender about the problem and asking for change than it is a question of somehow bringing oneself to forgive. It is only when an offense is genuinely past that it becomes a subject for forgiveness.

6) *"Forgive and forget" is not the best statement of the goal.* We do not usually forget what really hurt us or cost us a lot. Forgiving does not mean forgetting. What it does mean is that we let go of the offense so that we no longer use it as a reason for distance, a weapon to use against the other again when a new quarrel arises, or an excuse for our own bad behavior. Married couples sometimes hang on to their grudges and use them in these ways.

Holding a grudge is a powerful position. Forgiveness is an act of disarmament. We put our club away and make ourselves vulnerable to the other again. It is a real act of trust.

A prayer exercise that can help when forgiveness is difficult is to imagine the scene in which we were hurt, and then to imagine Jesus on the cross extending forgiveness to his enemies, and to move back and forth several times between the two scenes, asking for Jesus' spirit of forgiveness.

Good News: Two others who were criminals were led along with him to be crucified. When they came to Skull Place, as it was called, they crucified him there and the criminals as well, one on his right and the other on his left. Jesus said, "Father, forgive them; they do not know what they are doing." They divided his garments, rolling dice for them. (Lk 23:33–34)

Christian Action: Try with God's help to forgive someone who has hurt you. If it is a question of an ongoing wrong, talk the problem over with the person.

WEEK 3: SATURDAY

Being Sexual

One of the most mysterious and challenging aspects of being human is being sexual. From infancy right on through our last years, each of us is always and everywhere sexual whether we want to be or not. We find ourselves either male or female, homosexual or heterosexual, and our existence is profoundly shaped accordingly. Our sexuality is not just a fact; it is an energy. And as such it is often in our awareness clamoring to be dealt with. Does our Christian faith have anything to say about this facet of our humanity? We hope so, since it is so pervasive and dominant a dimension.

What the Christian churches have mostly said is: Beware, there are many ways to go wrong here. While there is truth in this, it does not seem like the first thing to be said about sexuality. Isn't the first and largest truth: Blessed are you, Lord, God of all creation! Blessed are you for the beauty and wonder of our sex organs and the depth and joy of our sexual experience. How great you are, how marvelous your designs! Thank you for giving us this tremendous gift. For if it is "spiritual" to contemplate mountain or sunset with praise in our hearts for the creator, it is surely no less spiritual to be aware of the marvel of our own bodies and of our coming together in love, and to feel the same wonder and gratitude. Are we not moved by beautiful flowers? Flowers are the sex organs of plants.

It is normal to be sexual. It is human. There is nothing bad about having a strong sexual interest and sexual fantasies. It is not wrong to feel sexual excitement. If we wanted to stop these occurrences, we could not. They belong to the way we are made, so we might as well relax and accept them. They are guiltless. The moral issue is, what are we going to *do* with our sexuality?

What is all this sexual energy? What is it for? It is part of the experience of our incompleteness, of our need for others. We are social beings in our very roots, and our sexual drive toward others is part of that yearning for fulfillment through togetherness. That is why our sexual urges are often strongest when we feel most lonely. They are telling us not so much that we need sex but that we need intimate relationships with people. Our drive toward sex is a dimension of our drive toward love. And our drive toward other persons is, at an even deeper level, our drive toward the Other. The mystery of sex and the mystery of God are intimately related.

It is love that satisfies, not sex. Love is the deeper need. Sex without love is pleasurable but rather empty, and usually leaves us feeling worse instead of better. But that does not mean that the sexual component of human loving has no real importance. We are physical beings, and we need to be touched and held. That is true not just for the infant, who dies without touch, but for the little child, and the adolescent, and the grownup, and the elderly person. All of us deeply need physical closeness and comforting through touch. It does not have to be genital.

A therapist once remarked that we need four hugs a day for

survival, eight for basic maintenance, and twelve for growth. A friend of mine told me that since there is no significant other in her life at this time, she goes regularly for a massage. She knows her need for touch, and in an appropriate expression of self-love gives herself this gift. A man I know who lives alone used to be afflicted sometimes during the night with anxiety attacks. He would wake up shaking, and could not go back to sleep. He learned that the attacks came when he was feeling distant from others. He started asking people for hugs at work on the days he was feeling that distance. Nobody refused him. In fact, everybody else seemed to appreciate the hugs as much as he did. His anxiety attacks stopped.

In the Christian perspective, the purpose of life is to learn how to love. Part of the task is to integrate that strong relational force we call sexuality into a genuine caring for ourselves and others. This is no easy task, for our sexuality presents itself as mere restless energy, powerful, tending often to be wayward, seductive, exploitive. Uncontrolled, it can hurt people. It needs to be tamed, humanized, integrated into our personhood. This is the work of years.

As we struggle with this, and everybody does, it is consoling to remember that God understands and supports us. It would not be like God to be focused on our sexual behavior, keeping count of our failures, waiting to punish. God is primarily interested rather in the much broader field of our loving, in the quality of our relating to all the people who come and go in our lives. As far as the gradual integration of sexuality into that loving is concerned, God watches, as any wise and loving friend would, with interest as well as with patience. God fully understands that we learn the more difficult things of life only gradually and by trial and error. Surely God forgives our mistakes in this area, as long as we make amends for how we may have hurt anyone and keep on trying to love authentically and responsibly.

Good News:

> *You have formed my inmost being, O God;*
> *you knit me in my mother's womb.*

I give you thanks that I am fearfully, wonderfully made;
wonderful are your works! (Ps 139)

Christian Action: Contemplate the wonderful gift of your sexuality today, and praise and thank God for it.

WEEK 3: SUNDAY

Eucharist

An important part of any retreat is the experience of daily eucharist. You probably came away from retreat with a renewed sense of the richness of the eucharist and a desire to attend more often. You may also have wanted to understand the eucharist better so that you could participate more fully and see the lines of relationship between this ritual and the rest of your life. Some of the following reflections may be helpful.

In the eucharist the risen Jesus is really present, in several different ways. He is present in the way he is incarnate in each person who is there. He is present in the words of scripture, in which he speaks to us. He is present in the symbolic reenactment of his dying and rising. He is present in the praying and worshiping activity of this community of people, all members of his body. And he is present as food and drink for us. Through our eucharistic encounter with him, his presence in us is strengthened so that we can more fully incarnate him in our lives in the world.

On this basis we can grasp what a great opportunity the eucharist is:

1) *It is an opportunity to hear and reflect on the word of God.* At least two scripture readings are proclaimed at each eucharist, with one of the psalms read between them. This is a chance to hear God's living word and to take it into oneself like bread or seed, so that our life can be more influenced by it.

2) *It is an opportunity to participate in the paschal mystery which illumines our existence.* At every eucharist there is a reen-

actment in symbol of the death and resurrection of Jesus. We remember and reflect on Jesus' act of generous self-giving, his surrender in trust to the suffering and death that result from his ministry, and the transformation of his death into new life by the power of God. This mystery of life coming out of death is the key to understanding our own existence, in which we too are constantly involved in various kinds of dying—through loss, suffering, labor, and growth—and in the transformation of our dying into new life by the power of God. At the eucharist we join our suffering and dying with those of Jesus in the same spirit of trust in God.

3) *It is an opportunity to be part of the body of Jesus Christ at worship.* All of us who belong to Jesus by faith and baptism are part of his body. At eucharist the body of Jesus gathers for worship. We see and greet one another. We pray and sing together. As we experience the support we give one another by our prayer and Christian example, we realize that none of us is alone in our struggle to be a follower of Jesus. In all the diversity of our particular personalities and life circumstances, we are one in the embracing love of Jesus and are joined with him in his worship of God. All together we are again missioned by him to the world.

4) *It is an opportunity to deepen our personal friendship with Jesus Christ.* In the eucharist Jesus feeds each of us personally with himself. His action brings back those scenes from his public ministry in which he fed multitudes of people with loaves and fishes after he had taught them God's word. Here it is his risen self that is given to us under the symbols of bread and wine, again after he has taught us God's word in the scripture readings and homily. There is a real person-to-person communing with him here in the sanctuary of our own hearts. This communing deepens our friendship with him.

> "You who feed on my flesh and drink my blood have
> everlasting life, and I will raise you up on the last day;
> for my flesh is real food, and my blood is real drink.
> You who feed on my flesh and drink my blood remain
> in union with me, and I in union with you." (Jn 6:54–56)

For all these reasons, the eucharist has always been the central ritual of the Christian community. It keeps the Christian vision and approach to life alive in our minds and hearts. It keeps the community together. And it strengthens the bond of friendship with Jesus Christ as the center and motivating force of our lives.

We cannot close without admitting that the eucharist as we actually experience it is not always all that it should be, and sometimes it leaves us feeling disappointed. What can we do when we feel dissatisfied with our parish liturgy? We can work to change it by offering our suggestions to the parish leadership, or by joining the liturgy committee and working for better worship. We can look around for a eucharist that better answers to our needs and desires. Or we can come to peace with our present liturgy and our worshiping community as they are with all their imperfections. If we do, it will probably be in the realization that nothing is perfect, and that this entire congregation, ragged though we be, are cherished by God.

Good News: By now they were near the village to which they were going, and he acted as if he were going farther. But they pressed him: "Stay with us. It is nearly evening; the day is practically over." So he went in to stay with them. When he had seated himself with them to eat, he took bread, pronounced the blessing, then broke the bread and began to distribute it to them. With that their eyes were opened and they recognized him; whereupon he vanished from their sight. They said to one another, "Were not our hearts burning inside us as he talked to us on the road and explained the scriptures to us?" They got up immediately and returned to Jerusalem, where they found the Eleven and the rest of the company assembled. They were greeted with, "The Lord has been raised! It is true! He has appeared to Simon." Then they recounted what had happened on the road and how they had come to know him in the breaking of bread. (Lk 24:28–35)

Christian Action: Focus on any one of the four dimensions of eucharist elaborated here. Use it as a way of participating more meaningfully in the eucharist today.

Appreciating Your Own Life

A married woman came in for counseling. She lamented her lot. She had several children, and they were very sloppy and left things lying around the house. They were loud too, and there was no quiet except when they were all gone. Her husband was as sloppy as the children, very forgetful, and clumsy besides. He broke things. The woman felt herself a total failure as a mother, and she hated Mother's Day above all feasts. She said she frequently found herself looking longingly over the back fence at the house of a neighbor woman who lived alone. How wonderful it must be, she thought, to have a place all to yourself, a place that is clean and quiet, a place where you have no one's laundry to do but your own.

At the same time as I was counseling this woman, another woman was coming too. She had never been married, and this was the great suffering of her life. Her dream had been to have a family, yet her time for childbearing was rapidly drawing to a close and there was no man. Everything else that made up her life seemed meaningless to her. One day she told me of the family that lived next door to her. Both the man and the woman were warm and wonderful people, and they had three beautiful children. It made her suffering all the greater to be living right next door to everything she had ever dreamed of yet for some reason had never had. Struck by the parable as well as by the coincidence, I looked up the two women's addresses. Sure enough, they lived next door to one another.

The temptation runs deep in human nature, particularly in some of us, to compare ourselves to others and come out the los ers. Other people seem to have everything; we have nothing. What is interesting about these comparisons is the way we go about them. We add up other people's assets; then we add up our deficits; then we compare. In areas where we are doing well, we make no comparisons. We simply take for granted all that is good in our lives, leaving our attention full scope to focus on what we do not have. Then we eat our hearts out.

If other people knew how we idealize their lives, it would undoubtedly make them laugh. They always have their own set of problems. At the bottom of this crazy game is our difficulty in loving ourselves and accepting life as it is. It is possible to spend years in the Never Never Land of fantasy. All the while we are gone our real yard grows more and more weeds from neglect.

The poet Edwin Arlington Robinson gave the problem immortal expression at the turn of the century.

> Whenever Richard Cory went down town,
> We people on the pavement looked at him:
> He was a gentleman from sole to crown,
> Clean favored, and imperially slim.
>
> And he was always quietly arrayed,
> And he was always human when he talked;
> But still he fluttered pulses when he said,
> "Good morning," and he glittered when he walked.
>
> And he was rich—yes, richer than a king,
> And admirably schooled in every grace:
> In fine, we thought that he was everything
> To make us wish that we were in his place.
>
> So on we worked, and waited for the light,
> And went without the meat, and cursed the bread;
> And Richard Cory, one calm summer night,
> Went home and put a bullet through his head.

The root of the problem of envy is negative thinking about ourselves and our lives. We forget that "God looked at everything that was made, and God saw that it was good." (Gen 1) We act as if in our case, God made junk.

How do we get healed? We ask God to heal us, and then we do our own part. We catch on to our negative patterns of thinking and stop them every time we become aware they are going on. We substitute positive belief statements for the negative ones, saying to ourselves many times during the day: "I am good. I am lovable. My life is worthwhile. I can be as happy as anyone." We stop idealizing other people's lives.

Each of us has from God all we need for what we are meant to be and do. Our life is a gift as it stands, a challenge and an opportunity. It is the only one we will ever have. The problem is not so much the hand we were dealt. It is our attitude.

Good News: Jesus said: *"You are my friends, if you do what I command you. I no longer speak of you as slaves, for a slave does not know what his master is about. Instead, I call you friends, since I have made known to you all that I heard from my Father. It was not you who chose me, it was I who chose you, to go forth and bear fruit. Your fruit must endure, so that all you ask the Father in my name he will give you. The command I give you is this, that you love one another." (Jn 15:15-17)*

Christian Action: Spend some time today prayerfully looking just at the good things about yourself and your life. Use these positive thoughts as the basis of a prayer of thanksgiving.

WEEK 4: TUESDAY

Praying with Scripture

Many people today are learning to pray with scripture and find the approach a very fruitful one. The remarks that follow might just confirm you in what you are already doing, or they may open a whole new avenue to God for you.

The key to praying with scripture is using your imagination. Take an incident from Jesus' life—for example, his healing of the leper. Imagine that you are in that scene, and it is happening right now. You can be the leper or Jesus or an onlooker who witnesses the interaction. If you are the leper you can ask Jesus to make you clean, and then feel him touch you and feel his healing power move through you. If you are Jesus, imagine yourself approached by someone who feels unclean and is looking for some kind of healing. How would you interact with that person? If you are an onlooker, you could watch how Jesus deals with the leper, and maybe you could have a talk afterward with the person who is healed or with Jesus or with both. You might discuss, among other things, who the leper is in today's society.

Scripture is written the way it is for exactly this purpose, that you can enter its scenes and have an actual encounter with God and/or with Jesus. For they live and are speaking and acting today in the ways scripture describes.

Jesus' teachings can be used for prayer in a similar way. One approach is simply to read some of his teachings slowly and reflectively in God's presence, letting them seep into your soul. You don't use the imagination so much, and you cover more material than you do when you are trying to imagine everything. But you are in no hurry. If you wish, you can use your imagination on the teaching. You can visualize Jesus actually teaching, the setting, the various types of people who are there, how Jesus looks and moves and speaks when he teaches, and how the various kinds of people present react to what he says. You can be in Jesus' audience yourself, and talk with people about the teaching, or take Jesus aside and discuss it with him.

No matter what passage of scripture you might be praying with, stay where you find something that touches you. This is important. Do not press on, trying to cover the whole text or to get many ideas or many images. What really nourishes your relationship with God is depth, not breadth, really assimilating something, not just getting acquainted with many things. When a particular image, or a line, or even a single word strikes and moves you, that is the place to rest, even if you spend your whole time of prayer there. In fact, if, when you begin to pray, you find yourself in immediate communion with God, stay with that and let the scripture text go.

People who pray with scripture sometimes worry that they may not be getting at what the passage really means, but might just be thinking their own thoughts. Is there any way to know when you are on track? Actually, there are many dimensions of meaning in a passage of scripture, not just one. The parables, teachings, and incidents from Jesus' life have different meanings for different people in various life situations. You've probably experienced that if you've ever discussed any given text in a group. If you are worried about "going off the deep end" in your interpretations, the best safeguard is to read scripture with other Christians, in the mainstream of the church. People working together can usually strike a balance.

We have looked at incidents from the life of Jesus and Jesus' teachings as material for prayer. His parables can also be used imaginatively for prayer. Take the parable of the good Samaritan, for instance. You can imagine yourself as the person who is mugged and hurt lying on the pavement, and experience yourself being helped by some passerby who owes you absolutely nothing. How would you receive it? You can be the good Samaritan. Imagine yourself really ministering to a complete stranger who has fallen on hard times. You can be the priest who walks on by. What are you so busy with, or so afraid of? What gives the parables their power is this entering into and experiencing them from the inside, not standing outside them and saying, Oh, I see the point. Some of the parables invite you to be something other than a person. You can imagine yourself as the seed, for instance, entering into dark and damp earth, and then gradually breaking open and beginning to grow into something new. What does that feel like? Are you willing to undergo the transformation?

Out of this discussion of ways of praying with scripture, a fresh insight may have come to you. Perhaps many of the ordinary experiences of your life are like parables with lessons in them. Sleeping and waking, being sick and getting well, washing your hands, having an argument and making up, eating, making love— perhaps these too are parables to attend to because they reveal something of the mystery of God.

Good News: And he said, "With what can we compare the kingdom of God, or what parable shall we use for it? It is like a grain of mustard seed, which, when sown upon the ground, is the smallest of all the seeds on earth; yet when it is sown it grows up and becomes the greatest of all shrubs, and puts forth large branches, so that the birds of the air can make nests in its shade." With many such parables he spoke the word to them, as they were able to hear it; he did not speak to them without a parable, but privately to his own disciples he explained everything. (Mk 4:30–34)

Christian Action: Take your favorite parable or incident from Jesus' life, and pray with it today.

WEEK 4: WEDNESDAY

How Could God Let This Happen?

A married woman in her thirties who had been sexually abused by her father for a year in her early teens had a conversation with God.

Jean: God, it is so hard for me to even talk to you about this. I've tried to bury it all these years, but it continues to eat at me deep inside. I guess I've always just felt that I am evil, because this happened. It went on for a whole year. I feel as though it was my fault.

God: Jean, it makes me happy that you want to bring this out into the open, and that you are talking with someone about it. I want to talk with you about it too. I am so sorry that it happened to you. It grieved me deeply at the time, and it still grieves me. Things like this really make me sad.

Jean: I had no idea you got sad. I didn't know you cared at all. I guess that's one reason why I haven't prayed to you very much. If you care the way you say you do, why did you let this happen?

God: I did all I could to prevent it. In fact, I am always trying

57

to prevent things like this from happening. I spoke to your father's heart many times, but he did not want to listen to me. When that happens, there isn't much I can do. You have children yourself, don't you, Jean? You know how it is when you try to get them to do what is good, and they won't do it? You are powerless, right? They are free.

Jean: But, God, you are much more powerful than I am. Surely there was something you could have done.

God: I know people say I am all-powerful. But I really am not. When I decided to create, I took a big chance. I made the decision to create a world that was really separate from me, and therefore genuinely free. It can go wrong in many ways, and it does. In fact, as you know, you people have the power now to destroy one another and the whole world utterly. I involve myself with all of you always, inviting you, persuading you, trying to lure you toward the good. That is all I can do. I send Jesus and other holy men and women as teachers and living examples.

Jean: You are different than I thought you were. I think I'm beginning to see it from your point of view. But, God, what can I do about this awful feeling I have about myself? I feel dirty, evil. So many times I've thought about what I could have done to prevent it from happening.

God: It wasn't your fault, Jean. I really want you to believe me when I tell you that. It is never the child's fault. It is always the adult's fault. It is easy for a woman in her thirties to think of things she could have done. At thirteen, you don't think of those things. You were terrified. He told you not to tell. And you were emotionally very needy at the time. He took advantage of that. It grieves me deeply. It was not your fault at all.

Jean: It helps to hear you say that. I just wish I could get rid of this terrible feeling inside. I've had it all these years. Will it ever go away?

God: It will gradually grow less now that you have begun to share it with others. They will tell you what I am telling you: you are not what you thought you are. You are good and beautiful, and I love you. Your goodness and beauty are much, much larger and deeper than the sexual abuse we are talking about. Much deeper. Much larger.

Jean: I will try to believe that.

God: Yes, Jean, it's true. You know, Jean, there really is evil in the world, and you are very aware of it because this happened to you. But, Jean, look at yourself. How did you turn out to be such a good person—someone who loves much, and tells the truth, and reaches out to others? The world cannot be all evil. There must be another mystery at work in it too, a mystery of graciousness, an energy that builds up and helps things grow. That mystery of graciousness is myself, Jean, quietly at work in the depths of things. I have a vision, and I have hope. And I will not give up on the world I am creating. Will you help me?

Jean: I will certainly try. I feel better now. Thank you.

Good News: Beloved, let us love one another, because love is of God; everyone who loves is begotten of God and has knowledge of God. The person without love has known nothing of God, for God is love. God's love was revealed in our midst in this way: God sent the beloved Son to the world that we might have life through him. . . . We, for our part, love because God first loved us. If you say, "My love is fixed on God," yet hate your sister or brother, you are a liar. If you have no love for the sister or brother you have seen, you cannot love the God you have not seen. The commandment we have from God is this: If we love God, we must also love our brothers and sisters. (1 Jn 4:7–21)

Christian Action: Make time today to talk with God about an area of your life where you question, "How could God let this happen?" If you need more help with it, talk with a friend or counselor.

WEEK 4: THURSDAY

Destroyed by Your Own Goodness

A woman came for spiritual direction who was deeply troubled. She was a counselor who spent a great deal of her free time working for peace and justice causes. She and her husband were aware of the plight of the poor and oppressed around the world and how the American standard of living contributes to their misery. What had brought on the inner turmoil now was their plans for a two week summer vacation back where family and friends lived. How could they justify the expense, given all the suffering in the world? She had gone back and forth in her mind for days, with increasing confusion, turmoil, and depression. She told her story with tears, seeing no way out.

In the *Spiritual Exercises* of St. Ignatius Loyola, a book which has served as the master plan for retreats since it was written over four hundred years ago, there is a very important principle for dealing with problems of this kind. St. Ignatius discovered it in the years immediately following his own conversion, when he was very earnestly seeking to do God's will in everything. The principle is that while evil people are tempted by what is morally evil, good people are more readily tempted by what seems morally good. The way the evil spirit works in good people is to destroy them by their own goodness, since temptations to evil do not interest them. So the evil spirit masks as a good spirit and invites such people to do something which seems good, such as being more humble, more generous, more self-sacrificing—pushing it to an extreme until they are depressed, burned out, or mentally ill.

The woman described above is clearly a good woman, very concerned about other people and wanting to do all that is right. But what if she decides not to take a vacation this year, next year, or for the next five years? What if every time she wants to buy an item of clothing for herself, go out to dinner, or see a movie, she says no in the interest of the poor? How long will she be able to do the good she is doing with her counseling and her labors on behalf of peace and justice?

In his own wrestling with issues of this kind, St. Ignatius became aware of a clear sign of the difference between the influence of the evil spirit and the good spirit inside of good people. The difference is in the feeling. The evil spirit, with its supposedly good and pious ideas, produces feelings of disturbance, sadness, confusion, and turmoil. The good spirit produces peace and joy—even when it moves us to do what is difficult. The woman described above is obviously in turmoil, confusion, and pain, a clear sign that it is not the good spirit that is suggesting she forego her vacation.

One sees the same pattern of temptation at work in the lives of mothers who put themselves so generously at the service of husband and children that they consider it wrong to ask anything for themselves. It shows up in retreatants who pray or fast excessively, and cannot peacefully continue the retreat. It snares good people who, in their desire to please God, become neurotically scrupulous and are always preoccupied with guilt. It deceives religious people who in their zeal end up condemning and even oppressing those who do not believe in the same way they do.

In all these cases, the course of action under consideration *seems* good. The two criteria which indicate that it is not *really* good are the inner turmoil and confusion that accompany it, and the destructive results to which it soon leads.

Good News: In contrast, the fruit of the Spirit is love, joy, peace, patient endurance, kindness, generosity, faith, mildness, and self-control. (Gal 5:22)

Christian Action: Recall a time when you have been deceived, or nearly deceived, by this kind of subtle temptation masquerading as an impulse from God. Now recall the feelings of peace and joy you had on a different occasion when God was clearly with you. Contrast the feelings. Note also the different kinds of results that followed from the actions you took under each impulse.

WEEK 4: FRIDAY

Grieving Your Losses

Retreat thoughts are not usually thoughts of grief. But before we are back into ordinary living for very long, our griefs are back too, for life has a good bit of grief in it. When a dear one dies, we grieve. When a significant relationship ends, we grieve. Grief is our reaction to any significant loss. We grieve when we lose a job, when something is stolen from us, when we move. We grieve when we lose health or vigor. It is not only losing what we had that affects us this way. We grieve for what might have been and will never be, for that is a painful loss too.

Let us reflect a bit on the process of grieving, and then see how a Christian faith perspective can help us get through it more gracefully.

In the course of our grieving, several different emotions sweep over us. Disbelief is one of them. Strong anger is another. A third is guilt, because we feel we should have been able somehow to prevent this. Fear is another, terror even, as we face the future stripped of what had become so important to us. And over all there lies a deep, deep sadness, keeping us often on the brink of tears. These emotions swirl around one another, now one, now another predominating. All are painful, and sometimes it seems there will never be an end.

But grief does come to an end—if we work it through. That is the marvel. The psyche works to heal itself. It has wonderful restorative powers within it, just as the body does. If we resist the temptation to try to push all our pain out of awareness, and just let the emotions swirl, accept them, share them with a trusted friend or counselor and with God, and live through each of them, we gradually come out the other side. During this time, we need to be especially kind to ourselves, asking less of ourselves than usual. We are just not up to our ordinary routine, and are quite fragile. It may take us a year or more to work our grief through, particularly when a very dear person has died or left us. But eventually we can arrive at acceptance. Acceptance does not mean that we never think again about what we lost, or miss it (even with tears); it is just that our existence is no longer dominated by grief. We move on, and begin to reconnect with the currents of life.

What light can Christian faith shed on this grieving process, which we seem to go through again and again as we live? It is part of the dying of Jesus and his rising again. All of our living is dying, and all dying is letting go. But always we rise to new life. In the end we will have to let absolutely everything go, and in total powerlessness surrender ourselves into the hands of God. And again, we believe, God will give us new life. All our griefs along the path of life are practice for that final event, opportunities for trust in God's mystery of death/resurrection.

When a man loses his wife, when a mother loses her child, it feels like the end of the world. What is the point of going on? What is there to live for? For a time, that is all one can feel, and one must feel it as part of getting through it. But then there is a clearing for faith. Can we let even this dear treasure go in trust, hoping against hope that God will somehow continue to give us life (who knows how?), perhaps even more life than we have had up until now? Can we move through our days in the world without clinging (yet passionately loving), looking to God for our daily bread one day at a time? Do we really believe that God is what God has always been—mystery of the future, always out in front of us, inviting us not to be afraid but to step forward into the new creation?

There is a saying: Life is what is happening to you while you are making other plans. There is a touch of humor in the saying, of cynicism even, yet there is a profound truth there. There is life as we imagine and plan it, and life as it actually unfolds. And always there is a gap between them. We need our plans, and we need our loves, and we are entitled to our griefs, but what we are ultimately involved in is a mystery deeper than any of these. The mystery is benevolent. Keeping focused on that, and trusting it, is what holds us together and brings us home.

Good News: None of us lives to ourself, and none of us dies to ourself. If we live, we live to the Lord; and if we die, we die to the Lord. Therefore whether we live or die, we belong to the Lord. For to this end Christ died and came to life again, that he might be Lord both of the dead and of the living. (Rm 14:7-9)

Christian Action: If you are in grief about something, let yourself grieve. Find a person in whom you have confidence and, in a series of conversations over time, share the experience, gradually working each of the feelings through.

Is It Ever O.K. To Hurt Someone?

I sat with a couple one time whose two-year marriage was on the rocks. Though they cared for one another, they felt very far apart. As we explored the problem, it came down to this: From the beginning, neither of them had communicated their irritations, dissatisfactions, or anger to the other as they occurred. They held it all in. The reason? They were good Christians. They did not want to hurt each other.

These are two people being destroyed by their own goodness. There is no Christian commandment not to hurt anyone's feelings. Nor is there a commandment not to feel frustration or anger at others. Jesus' commandment is to love others. Loving others well requires good judgment. How is love best expressed in a given situation? It might be by saying no to someone, and so disappointing them. It might be by telling someone a truth that will hurt their feelings. Love demands that we do nothing that will *harm* other people. But does hurting a person's feelings harm them?

One day Peter told Jesus he didn't think he should undergo suffering and death. And Jesus said to him: "Get behind me, Satan; because you think the way human beings think, not the way God thinks." (Mk 8:33) It is hard to imagine Peter feeling very good after that, especially since this exchange took place in the presence of all the disciples. Yet surely Jesus was not acting spitefully or vindictively toward Peter in expressing himself this way. He loved Peter and had his genuine good at heart.

One way of stating the Christian ideal is: Tell the truth with love. (Eph 4:15) Sometimes the truth hurts. And often that hurt can be very constructive in a person's life—fellow worker, friend, child, parent, spouse. How often have we ourselves been greatly helped in the long run by being told a truth that really hurt our feelings at the time?

In really close relationships such as marriage and deep friendship, sharing our true feelings, even the negative ones, is absolutely essential to the development of the relationship. Only if the other person *knows* our irritation, disappointment, or anger can the issues involved be addressed. Others cannot know unless we tell them. When the issues are addressed, either or both of us may hear a call to change. Quite the opposite happens when we spare one another's feelings. Neither of us grows, and the additional price we end up paying is the loss of intimacy, as happened to the couple described above.

How do we go about telling the truth with love? We express ourselves courteously and tactfully, with evident respect for the other person. We give a little thought beforehand as to how we will word it so that we keep the hurt to a minimum. We do not do it when we are angry. We concentrate on the outward behavior we would like to see changed rather than on possible inner motives, so that the other person does not feel as if we are mindreading, psychoanalyzing, or doing therapy. We speak in such a way as to make the problem seem smaller rather than larger than it really is, because this gives sufficient indication yet softens the blow. If we can think of good things to say about the person along with the painful truth, we definitely include those things, so that the person feels loved and appreciated, not just criticized. In short, we deal with the other person the way we would like to be dealt with ourselves.

It is not just hurting people's feelings that makes Christians hesitate to say what needs to be said in certain situations. Some feel an implicit prohibition against disappointing anyone, "letting them down," because that hurts too. How, for example, can we possibly say no to lonely people or needy people who ask us to be with them?

There are several legitimate Christian reasons for saying no. One is our own needs. Another is the needs of other people we love besides those making demands. Another is that it may not really be in the best interests of the lonely or needy persons that we carry so much of their burden. All three of these reasons for saying no are grounded in love. Disappointing people is not at all the same as harming them.

We might as well admit that it is not always the highest Christian motives that prompt us not to do what disappoints people or hurts their feelings. Sometimes we are simply afraid that the person we hurt or disappoint will think less of us or be angry at us, and that is too much for *us* to bear. And so, given the choice between doing what is genuinely good and acting so that we will enjoy everyone's approval, we choose to go for everyone's approval. That is a kind of slavery, the opposite of Christian freedom. What we lack is basic security and the courage of our convictions.

Good News: Let us speak the truth with love, and so grow up in all things into him who is the head, Christ. Through him the whole body grows, and with the proper functioning of the members joined firmly together by each supporting ligament, builds itself up in love. (Eph 4:15–16)

Jesus said: "If your sister or brother should commit some wrong against you, go and point out their fault, but keep it between yourselves. If they listen to you, you have won them over." (Mt 18:15)

Christian Action: If there is someone you have hesitated to speak truthfully with for fear of hurting their feelings or disappointing them, try today telling them the truth with love.

WEEK 4: SUNDAY

God of Play

Most of us take ourselves and our lives very seriously. We measure our worth by what we accomplish. We believe that to live is to produce, and by production to justify our existence. Christians especially, taking their cue from Jesus' total dedication to the welfare of others, pour themselves into their work, and feel guilty when they play.

Behind this approach to life often lies an image of God. God is seen as taskmaster, severe in appearance, concerned that every minute of our day be filled with purposeful activity. Perhaps this image of God is shaped, without our fully realizing it, by the way our earthly father and mother went about their lives, or by the teaching and example of a childhood Christian teacher.

Perhaps God is more many-sided than this image suggests. For if God has created beavers and ants, who seem to spend most of their time working, God has also created seals, dolphins, and seagulls, who seem to spend most of their time enjoying themselves. Human children do almost nothing but play for the first six years of life (and ask questions and get in and out of jams as they explore the world). Jesus tells us that in God's eyes we are all children, and that if we do not act as children we cannot enter the kingdom.

An image of God more akin to this spirit is contained in the following story:

A young mother takes her three young children to the seashore on a summer afternoon. While she sits and reads a short way off, her children play at the water's edge, building sand castles. When they are done they come to her and say, "Mother, come and see what we made!" So she goes with them. The oldest says, "Mother, look at my castle! It's the biggest. It has three towers and a wall!" And the mother says, "Very nice, dear." The next child says, "Mother, look at my castle! It even has a moat where the water comes in!" And the mother says, "I see it. That's very nice." The youngest points to a motley pile of sand and says, "Mother, look at my castle!" And the mother says, "It's beautiful, dear."

What does that mother want for her children? That they be safe. That they enjoy the sunshine, the fresh air, the summer day at the beach. She knows that the tide will come in and wash their castles away. She knows that this day will be absorbed into the number of all the days of their lives.

What does God want for us? That we be safe. That we enjoy the gift of life. That we be friends. And all the rest? All the projects we invest with such importance? God says, "Yes, dear. That's very nice."

Good News: A discussion arose among them as to which of them was the greatest. Jesus, who knew their thoughts, took a little child and placed it beside him, after which he said to them, "Whoever welcomes this little child on my account welcomes me, and whoever welcomes me welcomes the one who sent me; for the least one among you is the greatest." (Lk 9:46–48)

Christian Action: Keep an eye on the birds, fish, animals, and children for the next week. And give yourself the gift of one hour today to do something apart from your work, something you particularly enjoy.

Hard Choices

Sometimes we get ourselves into difficult situations. Or at least we find ourselves in them. Our job might be causing us a lot of distress. A relationship with a friend, a spouse, or a family member might be crushing us more often than it comforts or supports us. Fundamental disagreements about values in our local church might be causing us anger or disturbance much of the time. In all these situations people are involved, and Christians are supposed to be lovers of people. What does a Christian do in situations of this kind?

We have three basic options in any difficult situation. We can stay in it and work to change it. We can stay in it and learn not to let it bother us so much. Or we can remove ourselves from it. The guiding question for us as Christians is: Which is the most loving course of action, all persons considered? (That includes us.)

Before we decide either to accept a difficult situation as it is or to leave it, it seems good to see if we might be able to change it for the better. For the Christian vocation is to bring in the reign of God. What would this situation look like if God reigned in it? Maybe this conflict is an opportunity. Crisis time, after all, is growth time, for ourselves and possibly for others. Pain is a great teacher, and struggle stretches us and draws out some of the best of us. Maybe we can dialogue and work this situation through, and all of us will emerge a little more genuinely human. Perhaps I myself am a large part of the problem, and will learn something valuable here.

But sometimes we cannot change the difficult situation we are in. And for various reasons we cannot leave it. Then can we learn not to let it bother us so much? Can we let more roll off? Can we put the situation and the persons in it in broader perspective? Can we bear with it, and find life in other places? In this too there might be real growth for us, a toughening of the skin, a deepening of our patience, an enlargement of our love.

However, there are some situations in which our best course of action is to give up and withdraw. We cannot change the situation, we cannot come to peace with it, and it is gradually destroying us. Some relationships fall into this category. They are physically or verbally abusive, or there is simply no real caring or sharing in them. Some work or church involvements also fall here. There is real injustice, and the offending party has no interest in addressing it. Leaving the situation is not only an appropriate act of self-love; it makes a statement that may have a better chance of being heard than mere verbal protest and endurance.

Did Jesus ever give up on a situation? Yes, and sometimes he refused even to dialogue.

> The Pharisees came forward and began to argue with him. They were looking for some heavenly sign from him as a test. With a sigh from the depths of his spirit, he said, "Why does this age seek a sign? I assure you, no such sign will be given it!" Then he left them, got into the boat again, and went off to the other shore. (Mk 8:11–13)

With his disciples he made a different choice. He did not give up on them, but chose to keep working with their lack of understanding and courage rather than look for a whole new group. He seems not to have given up either on the religious leaders of his time. But he was not always gentle with them. He denounced them publicly on several occasions. Presumably there were many other situations which Jesus simply let go, not letting them bother him so much.

It is important to realize that as Christians we are not simply to put up patiently with everything. But in every situation we must be guided by love. The beatitudes express the spirit we would like to be ours.

How blest are the poor in spirit: the reign of God is theirs.
Blest too are the sorrowing; they shall be consoled.
Blest are the lowly; they shall inherit the land.
Blest are they who hunger and thirst for justice; they shall
have their fill.
Blest are they who show mercy; mercy shall be theirs.
Blest are the single-hearted, for they shall see God.
Blest too the peacemakers; they shall be called children of
God.
Blest are those persecuted for holiness' sake; the reign of
God is theirs.
Blest are you when they insult you and persecute you and
utter every kind of slander against you because of me.
Be glad and rejoice, for your reward is great in heaven;
they persecuted the prophets before you in the very same
way. (Mt 5:3–12)

Christian Action: Reflect on a difficult situation in your life. What is your most loving course of action, all persons considered? Take steps to follow that option.

WEEK 5: TUESDAY

Not Taking Yourself Too Seriously

There is a hazard connected with any important religious experience like a retreat. The hazard is pride, expressing itself as self-righteousness. It is one of those subtle temptations that creep up on good people unawares.

A religious experience gives rise to enthusiasm. Enthusiasm easily gives rise to dogmatism. Dogmatism says, ''This is *the* way. There is no other.'' We see this spirit sometimes in those who have found something wonderful in the charismatic renewal.

We see it in couples who have been greatly helped by Marriage Encounter or Cursillo. We see it in biblical fundamentalists whose lives have been turned around by their encounter with God's word. In each case there is a great enthusiasm which sometimes ends by shortening people's horizons.

"We have the truth, and you do not."
"We are right; you are wrong."
"We are of God; you belong to Satan."

The starting point is unmistakably good. There *has* been a genuine experience of God and an unmistakable enrichment of life. There *is* something good to share with others. But even good people are tempted, and this particular temptation plays to our innate tendency to make ourselves feel good by placing ourselves above others. We forget that we too are sinners—even after conversion and commitment. We lose sight of the fact that our every insight is only a partial insight, especially where religious matters are concerned. No one has the whole truth. No one has the only way. We overlook the largest fact of humankind's richly diverse religious history—that God is greater than any religious system, and draws people by many, many paths.

Self-righteousness effectively prevents us from seeing and hearing. There is no need to see or hear since we have the truth. We have come to *teach*. We smugly wait. When will they see the light and join us? How much we lose! We miss out on vast amounts of possible discovery and learning—not just about others, but about ourselves as well, for we can see ourselves clearly only in a perspective that includes other people's points of view. We lose even the opportunity we had to share our good news, because our arrogant attitude turns others away.

Jesus kept trying to *include*. He was sensitive to the good wherever he found it, and he found it in unlikely places—prostitutes, tax collectors, Samaritans, Gentiles. He promised that strange people would be found in the kingdom of God, while those who thought they were its children would find themselves outside it. The kingdom of God is a difficult place for those of us who must feel superior to someone to feel good about ourselves.

A wise person once said: Our first task in approaching another people, another culture, another religion is to take off our shoes, for the place we are approaching is holy. Otherwise we may find ourselves treading on another's dream. More serious still, we may forget that God was there before our arrival.

Good News: *Jesus then spoke this parable addressed to those who believed in their own self-righteousness while holding everyone else in contempt: "Two men went up to the temple to pray; one was a Pharisee, the other a tax collector. The Pharisee with head unbowed prayed in this fashion: 'I give you thanks, O God, that I am not like other people—grasping, crooked, adulterous—or even like this tax collector. I fast twice a week. I pay tithes on all I possess.' The other man, however, kept his distance, not even daring to raise his eyes to heaven. All he did was beat his breast and say, 'O God, be merciful to me, a sinner.' Believe me, this man went home from the temple justified but the other did not. For if you exalt yourselves you will be humbled; but if you humble yourselves you will be exalted." (Lk 18:9–14)*

Christian Action: Approach someone today whom you have tended to look down upon. Approach with reverence and a spirit of inquiry, to listen rather than to speak. See what you can learn from that person.

WEEK 5: WEDNESDAY

Sinful Systems

When slavery was part of life in the United States, most people simply took for granted that it was quite all right. It was assumed without question that black people were inferior to white people, that they could be captured and uprooted from their homeland and bought and sold as property. They could also be beaten or raped at the whim of their owners, and if one was killed, it was covered up and no one asked too many questions. That seems outrageous now, but only because we now stand outside the system. At the time, a great many Christians stood within it, their consciences untroubled.

The treatment of Jews in Nazi Germany is another example of a sinful system. Its horrors are well known. A whole nation participated, some people quite actively, many by passive acceptance. When those who actively participated were criminally charged after the war, their plea was: "We were just doing what we were told."

These examples give us a new insight into sin. We usually think of sin as a personal matter: I sin, other people sin. But over and above our personal sinfulness, there is the problem that sometimes we are joined together with other people in sinful systems. All of us cooperate in evildoing just by being part of the system. And usually we do not even advert to the fact that what we are doing is evil.

What are some of today's sinful systems? Though slavery is gone, racism is still very much alive, structured into our culture. Sexism is another of the pervasive evils of our culture, and of most cultures. Its assumption is that women are inferior to men, and should take their orders from men and fit into arrangements made by men. They work for less pay and are barred from many positions in church and economic life. Militarism is another evil seeded deeply in American culture. Instead of using our abundant resources to further life for all people in this country and the world, we put a huge percentage of it into armaments to protect our privileged way of life. We are willing to blot out millions of human beings with nuclear weapons if we have to. We are also the world's great supplier of weapons, often selling to both sides in the same conflict. Consumerism is another of our sinful structures. The American way of life, excessive in many ways, depends for its continuance on the systematic exploitation of poorer peoples and of the resources of the earth.

What makes systems sinful is that through them some people enjoy benefits at the expense of other people. Those other people are hurt, hindered, violated, sometimes destroyed. Thus sinful structures are the opposite of love, and run contrary to God's purpose for humankind. Jesus' call to discipleship is not just a call to turn away from personal sin. It is a call to work with God in changing human society so that God truly reigns in it. The marks of God's reign are justice, peace, and joy for the entire human community.

That may sound inspiring, but the work of changing systems is arduous. What makes it so difficult to stand up against an evil system is that almost everyone is involved in it, including our relatives and friends. Besides, the system is firmly established and very powerful, and we are rewarded for going along and penalized for going against.

So where do we begin? Probably the first thing is to pray to be healed of our blindness so that we recognize sinful systems and our connivance in them. It is not very responsible to believe that whatever the corporation, the government, or the church chooses to do is good. Such a stance is both naive and lazy.

When we recognize structural sinfulness our duty is to stop cooperating with it as far as we can. It is to speak out against it, though that may require much courage. It is to work to change it, though the labor may be long and unrewarding. It is sometimes to leave the system, though that is usually very risky. All this adds up to considerable personal cost, which is why sinful structures usually enjoy long existence and abundant membership.

And so our consideration starts with sin and ends with discipleship. This kind of discipleship can only be sustained by prayer and the support of a community.

Good News: Jesus told them a parable: "Once there was a rich man who dressed in purple and linen and feasted splendidly every day. At his gate lay a beggar named Lazarus who was covered with sores. . . . " (Lk 16:19)

Jesus said: "O Jerusalem, Jerusalem, murderess of prophets and stoner of those who were sent to you! How often have I yearned to gather your children, as a mother bird gathers her young under her wings, but you refused me." (Mt 23:37)

Christian Action: Are there any ways in which your silence or your actions strengthen sinful systems in your workplace, neighborhood, or church? What do you think God's call to you in any of these situations is?

WEEK 5: THURSDAY

How Much Is Enough?

A married woman found herself in the position of best friend and closest support to her widowed mother, who lived in an apartment across town. The mother was lonely and needy, and wanted her daughter there all the time. No matter how much time the daughter spent with her at her apartment or on the phone, it was never enough.

For another woman, it was her widowed father who lost all interest in living when his wife died, put off all friends, quit his ordinary activities, and waited for his daughter's daily visit so he could talk about how bad it was and cry with her.

All of us face situations like this from time to time, even if they are not as dramatic. It may be the demands that spouses and children make, the way people put upon us at work, the sorts of inexhaustible needs certain friends present. This poses a dilemma for the Christian, who has been told many times to love and serve others and to sacrifice in the process. What does this mean? Is the Christian simply at the beck and call of others, to be used and abused until finally released by a merciful death?

One of the unfortunate things about the gospels is that they are so brief and hence so selective in what they portray of Jesus. They show us very little of how he set limits. We could use more sketches of Jesus at play, Jesus at rest, and Jesus saying no, just to balance off the picture of his generosity. He must have set limits or he could not have survived as long as he did. For in this world of suffering humanity, the work of the compassionate helper is never done.

Whether we consider the life of the Christian helper generally devoted to service, or the life of the individual faced with a particular challenge of the sort described above, there have to be some guidelines for deciding how much is enough:

1) When I find myself often exhausted, irritable, or depressed, I am attempting too much. My own needs are not being met, and I am not the only one who suffers the consequences. Those around me do too, including those I am supposedly helping.

2) Since Christian service is endless, I had better pace myself. It is a marathon I am in. I had better take it a little easier, so I can go all the way. The good I can do steadily over a lifetime is much greater than the good I can do with that reckless generosity that forces early retirement.

3) A pointless sacrifice is just that: pointless. Sometimes sacrifices I make for others really help them or make them happy. That is a meaningful sacrifice. But sometimes it does not seem to do any good at all, as in the case of those people for whom it is never enough. It just seems to go down the drain—and it costs me a lot. When I am not saving anyone else's life, it seems that I might as well at least save my own.

4) Sometimes what I am inclined to do for others is not really good for them. Take the two cases above, the lonely older people. Is it really helpful to them in the long run that I am willing to try to fill the void in their lives? Or would they grow more if they had to do more for themselves, really face themselves, develop a broader network of friendships, create other ways to fill their days? I have to beware of my tendencies to rescue.

5) Even the Christian has rights. If the Christian works out of Jesus' motive, "I have come that you might have life and have it more abundantly," then under God the Christian has that same right to the gift of life. It is a fair bet that if Jesus came upon someone who was exhausted in the service of others, he would not simply commend the person's largeheartedness. He would say, "My friend, you need a break," even as he said to his own disciples, "Come apart and rest awhile." (Mk 6:31)

Particularly prone to excess of self-giving are women, so conditioned to take care of others and ask nothing for themselves. Also prone are those who grew up in families in which one or both parents were unequal to their task, and the children were prematurely thrust into positions of responsibility. No one ever asked these children, ''What do *you* need? Now as adults they hardly know what their needs are, and they feel guilty when they ask for anything. What such persons need to hear is the healing message that God is a God of life for all. They are precious too.

Good News: *"Can a mother forget her infant, be without tenderness for the child of her womb? Even should she forget, I will never forget you. See, upon the palms of my hands I have written your name." (Is 49:15–16)*

   "I am the Lord, your God, the Holy One of Israel, your savior. I give Egypt as your ransom, Ethiopia and Seba in return for you. You are precious in my eyes and glorious, and I love you." (Is 43:3–4)

Christian Action: Be good to yourself today. Go to a movie, walk in a beautiful place, treat yourself to a massage. Do it out of the conviction that you are loved and God's gift of life is meant for you too.

WEEK 5: FRIDAY

Healing Memories

Our lives can be greatly hampered by painful experiences from the past which still live deep inside us. The painful experience may have been sexual or physical abuse at home, lack of parental love, hurtful encounters with peers, loss of a loved one through death or rejection, or anything else that left us deeply self-doubting, guilty, insecure, or afraid. Such experiences often continue to affect the way we feel about ourselves, the way we respond to life's opportunities, and the way we relate to other people. Sometimes they also hinder our relationship with God. In any case they are of concern to God, who loves us and wants us to be free and happy.

We cannot heal ourselves. We need God and other people to help us. The process of healing involves several steps.

1) *Sharing the pain.* A pain must be heard to be healed. We have to share our painful memory, reliving it as we do. This means really letting the awful feelings come back, frightening though they be, and openly sharing them with someone we trust. The person has to be willing and able to let us crumble momentarily, if that happens, as we reencounter our deep hurt, anger, guilt, sorrow, despair or whatever the feelings may be. We have to be able to discharge these feelings for our healing. We may well need to do this several times, as our memories tend to come back piece by piece rather than all at once when we open the long-closed door.

2) *Finding the hidden blessing.* We are well aware of the dreadful side of our painful memories. We are usually much less aware that God was working with us in the tragedies of our lives to bring some good out of them. Getting free of the pain depends on our bringing this positive aspect of misfortune into awareness. For example, people lonely in childhood often develop a deep relationship with God. People who are not well cared for often develop independence and personal resourcefulness. People who suffer much often learn compassion for the sufferings of others and end up ministering to them in some way. What are the blessings God has drawn out of some of the difficult experiences of your life? Perhaps a friend can help you name them.

3) *Forgiving the person who has hurt us.* This is usually very difficult, and we need to ask God's help. In prayer, we try to see those who hurt us in their context at the time. Maybe they did the best they could with what they had. A man in his forties forgave his father for never spending any time with him as a child when he learned how the father had been raised by his father. A woman in her thirties was able to forgive her mother for divorcing her father, when she came to a point in her own marriage where she saw divorce as her only option. This underscores the truth that forgiveness often takes time, and we need to be patient with ourselves. Often we have to be some distance from the event, and to

have gotten our lives back on track before we can forgive. We may still feel some hurt after forgiving; nevertheless we have basically let go of our hostility, and stopped using the injury either as a weapon or as an excuse.

4) *Putting the whole process in the context of prayer.* Each of the steps outlined above is difficult, and we need God's help. We often need God's support to have the courage to face our pain and share it with someone else. We need God to enlighten our understanding so that we can see how the struggles, tragedies, and deprivations of our lives have paradoxically blessed us. We need God's touch to soften our hearts so that we can forgive those who have hurt us. Our friends can help us with all of this too, not only praying for us, but praying with us as well.

It makes no sense to carry painful memories around un-healed. They lock us into bitterness and paralysis. God will heal and free us if we really want it. But we have to be willing to face the pain, and then let go.

Good News: Who will separate us from the love of Christ? Trial, or distress, or persecution, or hunger, or nakedness, or danger, or the sword? . . . In all this we are more than conquerors because of the one who has loved us. For I am certain that neither death nor life, neither angels nor principalities, neither the past nor the future, nor powers, neither height nor depth nor any other creature, will be able to separate us from the love of God that comes to us in Christ Jesus, our Lord. (Rm 8:35–39)

Christian Action: Reflect and see if there are any painful memories inhibiting your life. With the help of a trusted friend, try to arrive at some healing of one of these memories, using the steps suggested above.

Simplicity of Life

Julie made a very significant retreat a month ago, and has pursued the Christian life very seriously since. Looking over her situation now, she finds one matter she is still not settled about. She turns to God in prayer.

Julie: I have a question for you, God. Our retreat director gave a talk on Christian transformation. He said our lives are made up of four main relationships, and we should keep working to make them more and more Christian. I feel as if I have made some progress in my relationship to you, to myself, and to other people. The one I can't figure out is my relationship to things. In fact, I can't even remember what he said we were supposed to do about that one.

God: You really are doing beautifully in those first three areas, Julie. I appreciate your growing interest in the fourth. What is important in your relationship to things is that you keep your life simple, that you not get caught up in acquiring more and more things, as many of your friends and neighbors are. The reason is that you cannot do that and still have a heart that is really interested in me and my work in the world.

Julie: I'll be honest with you, God. It is really hard for me to hear what you are saying. I like things. Why can't I have them?

God: You can have a lot of what you want, Julie. You are certainly entitled to what you need and a few other things besides. I am talking about getting caught up in a whole way of life where getting rich becomes the most important goal in life, where clothes are a real preoccupation and you shop a lot, where you want a bigger house and another car and maybe a summer place with a boat, and a vacation in the South Sea islands. In your country today, many people are racing toward those goals. I already mentioned the problem of how it ties up all your interest and energy. The other problem with it is the way it affects the rest of the human community.

Julie: I can see better what you mean now. I do have some tendencies in that direction. But what do you mean about the human community?

God: Let me paint you a picture. Suppose the whole world were a single village of a hundred people. Suppose six people in that village possessed forty percent of the goods available, while the other ninety four people possessed the remaining sixty percent. That probably wouldn't seem very fair to the ninety four especially since the goods of the village are not distributed equally among them either, but some people have much more than they need while others do not have the bare necessities of life.

Imagine the housing in the village. There are six mansions, some brick houses, some woodframe houses, and many shanties. And there are a large number of people, certainly more than six, who do not have any home at all but live and sleep in the streets. Some people in the village eat and drink sumptuously, while many are hungry and their children cry for food. Many are sick, but they have no money for medical care. The fathers and mothers of these families look at the mansions of the rich, and they are consumed with anger. They *work* for those people, but are not paid enough to live on. They would like to storm their homes and take what they need, but the mansions of the rich are surrounded by high walls and guarded by police. In fact, the rich spend more on protection than it would cost to feed, clothe, and shelter all the poor—much, much more.

I've painted you a sad picture, but that is the world I see everyday. I hear the cries of the poor. And the six people with the forty percent of the wealth are the people of the United States, just six percent of the population of the world.

Julie: That makes me feel awful. I don't know what to do.

God: I know you did not set out to make the world this way, nor did your parents or their parents. But this is the situation that has developed, and it is clearly a very unjust system, harmful to many people. That is why economics and politics are such central concerns of mine and of all people who want to help me accomplish my purpose.

Julie: Now I understand better why Jesus talked so much about riches and poverty. He really championed the poor, and called the rich to social responsibility. You've given me a much better idea how to think about my relationship to things. You've laid a heavy task on me too where economics and politics are concerned.

God: I don't want you to try to carry all that alone. And there is only so much you can do to bring about change. But each person's contribution to the effort counts. The reign of God is like a mustard seed that grows, you know.

Julie: I know. You've given me an awful lot to think about. I guess I'll just have to spend some time with it. Thanks, God.

Good News: Jesus said, "Do not lay up for yourselves treasure on earth. Moths and rust corrode; thieves break in and steal. Make it your practice instead to store up treasure in heaven, which neither moths nor rust corrode nor thieves break in and steal. Remember, where your treasure is, there your heart is also." (Mt 6:19–21)

Christian Action: Do one thing today that shows you are more interested in the reign of God than in acquiring things for yourself— for example, donate to a food bank, help work on a justice or peace project.

WEEK 5: SUNDAY

Friendship with Jesus Christ

Sometimes Christian discipleship seems very hard. We aspire to reach the high ideals Jesus taught. We try to imitate his sublime example. We do not succeed at either, and it feels exhausting. Is that all discipleship is: just aspiration and imitation, with poor success? No, fortunately it has another dimension as well, one that is far easier. That dimension is friendship with Jesus Christ. It is a free gift. He offers himself to each of us as companion, and being his disciple means being his friend.

If you love me you will be true to my word, and my Father will love you. We will come to you and make our dwelling place with you. (Jn 14:23)

Here I stand knocking at the door. If you hear me calling and open the door, I will enter your house and dine with you. (Rev 3:20)

No longer do I call you servants; I have called you friends. (Jn 15:15)

And know that I am with you always, even till the end of the world. (Mt 28:20)

Friendship with Jesus Christ resembles our ordinary human friendships in many ways. It means being present to each other in love, and exchanging with each other what each has to give. It is also somewhat different. For one thing, Jesus is not physically present the way our friends are. He does not touch us as they do, nor give us clear verbal messages. Nor can we see and touch him as we would like to. This makes relating harder. We have to rely on faith, *believing* in his presence and love. We also have to use our imaginations, trying to picture him in some way, perhaps even visualizing ourselves and him in interaction.

There is another important difference in this friendship, a welcome one: This is a friendship we can count on no matter what. It will not suddenly end—unless *we* want to end it. He will be faithful and will stick with us even through all the wanderings and mistakes that mark our lives. There is no "last straw" with him, as there is with some of our other friends. Forgiveness and reconciliation are always extended. Nor need we fear separation by geography or death. Jesus goes with us wherever we go.

St. Paul's whole life is based on friendship with Jesus Christ. "For me, to live is Christ," he says. (Gal 1:21) If we read his letters, we notice how he turns his whole life over to Christ, trusts him, asks him for what he needs, conceives his whole lifework in terms of him, and gratefully receives the constant love of Christ as his sustenance. "He loved me, and gave himself up for me," he exclaims. (Gal 2:20) Paul's oft repeated description of the Christian life is life "in Christ." Paul is a fine example of that type of existence Jesus describes in his farewell discourse:

> I am the vine, you are the branches. If you live in me and I in you, you will produce abundantly; for apart from me, you can do nothing. (Jn 15:5)

Paul puts it this way: "I can do all things in him who strengthens me." (Phil 4:13) Many of the other saints as well have experienced and described this sort of intimate relationship. Perhaps you had a taste of it yourself on your retreat, and want to keep it alive now that retreat is over.

What do we do to deepen and strengthen friendship with Jesus Christ? Nothing more than continue to ask for it and open our hearts to it. But we must seriously want Christ in our lives. We have to be willing to turn ourselves over to him in trust and obedience, as he turned himself over to the Father in trust and obedience. And we have to cultivate the friendship through the exercise of sharing. Then it will grow, and we ourselves will grow—into the image of the one we love.

So when discipleship seems difficult, let us remember this other dimension of it, and draw comfort from the friendship that lies at the heart of what we are living.

Good News: May Christ dwell in your hearts through faith, and may charity be the root and foundation of your life. Thus you will be able to grasp fully, with all the holy ones, the breadth and length and height and depth of Christ's love, and experience this love which surpasses all knowledge, so that you may attain to the fullness of God. (Eph 3:17–19)

Christian Action: Talk today with the Christ who is with you. Share your life with him. Let him love you. And ask that the friendship keep deepening.

WEEK 6: MONDAY

Who Am I?

Until I can answer four questions in most situations I find myself in, I am not yet a person. The four questions are: What do I think? What do I feel? What do I need? What do I want? In answering them, I express my personhood. If I cannot answer them, I do not yet know who I am.

What is surprising is that a lot of people are unable to answer them. Their lives are governed by what other people think, feel, need, or want. They do not really have a life of their own, though they may think they do, and the root of their difficulty is the lack of a self.

I remember a young woman in counseling who was in a stormy relationship with a man. It was clear from her reports that she was unhappy in it much more often than she was happy. When I asked her what she thought was causing the problems in the relationship, she didn't know. When I asked her what she needed in the relationship, she didn't know and so could not ask for it. When I asked her why she was staying in it, she didn't know that either. She was thoroughly confused. It emerged that this happened to her in all her relationships with men. She lost herself in relationship every time, because she did not know who she was and just tried to adapt to whatever he seemed to be.

Women are particularly prone to letting themselves be defined by other people. Men often do not know what they feel. This has to make God wince, because it robs women and men of so much of their dignity as human persons. God wants life for us. How can we live full and satisfying lives if we do not claim our selfhood, and how can we do that if we do not know who we are?

How can we develop more selfhood?

I feel. Our feelings are an elaborate information system, telling us how we are in any given situation. Knowing what we feel and sharing our feelings effectively with others has a great deal to do with our own development and the measure of control we have over our lives. A good exercise for those who often do not know what they are feeling is to do a sort of "probe" of their inner consciousness several times a day, seeking what they are feeling in various situations.

I think. This one is harder in some ways. Developing thoughts that are really ours requires accurate information and clear reflection. Stating what we think often takes courage. But if we do not have independent judgment and the courage of our convictions, we can hardly call ourselves persons. Letting the TV set tell us what to think, or listening in groups and then agreeing with the prevailing voice, scarcely qualifies us as selves.

I need. Listening to our feelings and thoughts usually tells us what we need. The hard step for many of us is asking for what we need. At the root of the difficulty often is a doubt that we have any right to get our needs met. But everybody has a right to get his or her needs met. Look what happens if we do not get our needs met: we develop headaches, backaches, ulcers, alcoholism, depression. Making our needs known and taking appropriate action to get them met seems the better alternative. Other people usually do not know what our needs are, and sometimes they do not care very much. Getting our needs met has to be a matter of personal responsibility.

I want. What do I want from life? What do I want from this relationship? What do I want in this situation? Again feeling and thinking are the key to knowing this, and appropriate assertiveness is the means of bringing it about. What hinders? Sometimes the fear of what others might think, especially if what I want differs from what most people seem to want. Another hindrance is a common Christian doubt: Do I have a right to want anything? Yes, if it is good and my claiming it does not harm anyone. Why not? Surely life is a gift to be enjoyed.

The great Swiss psychiatrist, Carl Jung, says that the life project before each of us is to become the person it lies within us to be and to live out our individual destiny as it unfolds. We find our personhood by listening to our feelings, watching our fantasies, attending to our dreams, reflecting on our experience, listening to the feedback other people give us. We develop our personhood by the expressing and acting out of what we are learning about ourselves. The process is exciting, adventuresome. In cooperation with God, each of us creates a unique self.

Jesus was a self. He knew what he thought, what he felt, what he needed, what he wanted. He expressed it and acted out of it. Some people approved. Others emphatically did not. He let that be as it might. Rooted in God, he wanted only to be as fully as possible the person it lay within him to be and to live out his unique destiny as step by step it unfolded. Practically everyone who has come to know something of him has admired him. He was a person.

Our scripture passage today shows us three different persons making choices which shape their identities.

Good News: On their journey Jesus entered a village where a woman named Martha welcomed him to her home. She had a sister named Mary, who seated herself at the Lord's feet and listened to his words. Martha, who was busy with all the details of hospitality, came to him and said, "Lord, are you not concerned that my sister has left me to do the household tasks all alone? Tell her to help me." The Lord in reply said to her: "Martha, Martha, you are anxious and upset about many things; one thing only is required. Mary has chosen the better portion and she shall not be deprived of it." (Lk 10:38–42)

Christian Action: Beginning today, ask yourself the four questions in various situations in which you find yourself. Develop your sense of selfhood. Try acting out of it more.

Hearing God's Call

A woman in her late twenties once asked me to help her discern whether she had a religious vocation or not. Did God want her to be a sister? She had puzzled over it for years without being able to resolve it. Her question was: How do you know when you have a vocation?

I said: We all have a vocation and for all of us it is the same: to live as Jesus did, to base our lives on love. Being a sister or lay person, being single or married—these are just different social contexts for doing that. Speaking as if some Christians have vocations and some do not reflects a strange way of looking at things.

O.K., she said. But does God want me to be a sister? So I asked: What do you most deeply want to do with your life? She wondered what difference *that* made. It was not a question of what she wanted, but of what *God* wanted. I said: When you have found what you most deeply want, you will have found what God wants for you.

This came as quite a surprise to her. So I developed the idea further. God's will for you is contained within your own personhood. It is God who made you who you are, and what God wants for you is contained in who you are. If you are looking for God's will for you, listen carefully to your own deepest wants.

But isn't it irresponsible to be guided by what we want? she asked. Don't we sometimes want what is bad for us and against God's will?

I am talking about deep and persistent levels of wanting, I explained, not about what a person might feel like under an impulse. "I feel like retiring in my early thirties." "I feel like punching you in the nose." "Sometimes I feel like leaving my marriage." I am talking about a more serious quantity, what persists at a deep level when we have considered all things carefully. Naturally, I am talking also about what is in the realm of possibility, not about what lies outside our control (for example, marrying a person who does not want to marry us, bringing someone who has died back to life). And I am presuming something: that the person I am dealing with is, like the woman described here, basically oriented toward the good. They genuinely want their lives to be in harmony with God. The very fact that someone is asking about God's will is sufficient indication of that orientation.

I find that people sometimes have trouble knowing what they really want. I suggest different ways of getting at it. Watch your daydreams. Watch your night dreams too. In both, deep levels of the psyche often reveal themselves. Notice what sorts of living examples catch your attention and enthusiasm, people who make you say: I want to be like that; I want to do what that person does. Sometimes we meet such people through stories rather than actual contact. You can also tease out what is inside you by journaling every day, writing about your inner thoughts and feelings with special attention here to the direction of your wanting.

The woman in the story spent some time reflecting on what she really wanted to do with her life, and reached a peaceful negative decision on religious life. A different decision was made by a priest who had fallen in love with a woman and was considering marriage. I suggested the same fundamental approach. After prayerful reflection he realized that he most deeply wanted to remain the priest he was, and he ended the relationship.

Good News: *With what shall I come before the Lord and bow before God most high? Shall I come before God with holocausts, with calves a year old? Will the Lord be pleased with thousands of rams, with myriad streams of oil? Shall I give my firstborn for my crime, the fruit of my body for the sin of my soul?*

You have been told, O child, what is good, and what the Lord requires of you. This is what Yahweh asks of you, only this: To live justly, to love tenderly, and to walk humbly with your God. (Micah 6:6–8)

Christian Action: Notice today those people in your life or in stories you hear who make you say: I want to be like that. What does this tell you about your own deepest wants?

Overcoming Addictions

Most of us probably do not think of ourselves as addicts. We're not on drugs, and we don't get drunk very often. But is it that simple? Addiction is subtle. Drugs and alcohol do have a grip on a lot of us—even where the drugs are of the prescribed variety. Food is the unmanageable substance for a great many others, whether we starve ourselves (anorexia), binge regularly, or combine such binges with purging (bulimia). Some of us are addicted to sex. Others are slaves to destructive relationships, have great difficulty leaving them, and leave one only to enter another. Some of us are addicted to buying things, and go shopping when we are not feeling just right. Others are addicted to television, and spend all our non-working hours in front of the tube. Others are addicted, perhaps with equal profit, to sleep.

What all addictions have in common is that with respect to the addictive substance, whatever it is, we are not free. It has a powerful hold on us, and it controls us instead of we controlling it. What is worse is that no matter how comforting the substance is at times, the dance we are locked into with it is in one way or another a dance of death. Our partner is destroying us. Our possibilities for fullness of life are seriously diminished by this one consuming unfreedom.

How is addiction a spiritual concern? Almost always, someone (besides ourselves) is being hurt by our addiction. And there is the hurt to ourselves, the slow self-destruction. God's wish for us and for everyone else is always life, abundant life. (Jn 10:10) These are the chief reasons why addiction is an evil. Then, if we heed God's call to come out of our prison, other spiritual issues will come into play. It will take humility to ask for the help we need, and we do need help. Very rarely can anyone triumph over the power of an addiction without steady support from other people. Many people say they die a kind of death in admitting to another person that something in their lives has become unmanageable. It will take courage to explore the underlying emotional problems which contribute to our addiction. It will take perseverance and hard work to make the changes we will have to make. It will take prayer and trusting dependence on God to be healed and set free.

Objectively speaking, an addiction is a kind of idolatry, a reliance on something other than God for life and happiness. Subjectively speaking though, one's real guilt in the idolatry is very difficult to assess, since there is so much unfreedom. When we are addicted, we usually feel much guilt and berate ourselves. We try again and again to break out by an act of the will. It does not work, because a disease of some kind, not a weak will, is at the root of the problem. What we do have the power to do is to acknowledge that there is an insurmountable difficulty and ask for help. That, of course, involves dying a death.

But in human existence, graced as it is by God's love, where there is death there is resurrection. An addiction can turn out to be a great blessing. Not that God sends us our addictions, but God is there to help us overcome them and lead us out into freedom and expansion of life. In wrestling with those things that would destroy us we grow into the fullness of our humanity, and usually experience a deeper insertion into human community in the struggle.

Good News: *Rejoice in the Lord always! I say it again: Rejoice! Everyone should see how unselfish you are. The Lord is near. Dismiss all anxiety from your minds. Present your needs to God in every form of prayer and in petition full of gratitude. Then God's own peace, which is beyond all understanding, will stand guard over your hearts and minds, in Christ Jesus.*

Finally, sisters and brothers, your thoughts should be wholly directed to all that is true, all that deserves respect, all that is honest, pure, admirable, decent, virtuous, or worthy of praise. Live according to what you have learned and accepted, what you have heard me say and seen me do. Then will the God of peace be with you. (Phil 4:4–9)

Christian Action: Reflect prayerfully today on whether some addiction, blatant or subtle, might be at work in your life. Is there some action you need to take?

WEEK 6: THURSDAY

Peaceful Acceptance

It seems that each of us has some difficult thing we have to accept in life. We don't want it at all, but there it is. It may be an unwanted pregnancy. It may be a burdensome person we have to take care of. It may be the psychic damage of our childhood, or some galling personal limitation. For one man I know, it was his physical deformity; for a woman, her epilepsy. For a married man, it was his wife's lack of interest in sex. For a married woman, it was her husband's inability to share emotionally and spiritually. Many people I have known have had to accept the loss of a very dear person and somehow go on.

As we know, not everything that befalls us is God's will by any means, and our first response to suffering ought to be to resist and overcome it if we can. Yet for everyone there seems to be some unsolved remainder, some painful burden we just cannot shake off. What do we do?

It is all right to be angry about it, and to speak that anger very honestly to God as many people in the bible do. It is all right to grieve. Such grieving is not only appropriate but therapeutic. It is all right to share our burden from time to time with someone who understands and supports us. Life is not meant to be lived in isolation.

What is not Christian, and not helpful, is to spend our whole lives in bitterness or self-pity, envying and resenting others because they do not suffer as we do. Actually, we do not know what they suffer, for people are like icebergs, one-tenth above the surface, nine-tenths below. And bitterness and self-pity do not take our pain away. They just keep us on the sidelines of the great game of life.

A priest once told me that every time he was let deeply into someone's life, he became aware of a crucifixion going on in that person's heart. He said the two different responses he saw people make to that were well exemplified in the thieves who were crucified on either side of Jesus. One cursed and blasphemed Jesus. The other prayed, "Lord, remember me when you come into your kingdom." (Lk 23:39–43)

The secret of life, it seems, is to focus not on what we do not have but on what we do have, and to make the most of it. We all know people who have very little, yet seem to be happier than those who have much more.

And what of our painful burden? It always contains some blessing. The patriarch Jacob once found himself wrestling all night with a mysterious being, and he came away wounded in his hip joint. But he also came away blessed and knew that his struggle had somehow been with God. (Gen 32) Paul suffered from some "thorn in the flesh," and frequently prayed to be rid of it. God answered him: "My grace is sufficient for you; for strength is made perfect in weakness." (2 Cor 12:9) Perhaps someday we will thank God for our struggles, our sufferings, even our sinfulness, for we will see that our wrestling with them has made us the persons we are.

Good News: In the course of that night, Jacob arose, took his two wives with the two maidservants and his eleven children, and crossed the ford of the Jabbok. After he had taken them across the stream and had brought over all his possessions, Jacob was left there alone. Then some man wrestled with him until the break of dawn. When the man saw that he could not prevail over him, he struck Jacob's hip at its socket, so that the hip socket was wrenched as they wrestled. The man then said, "Let me go, for it is daybreak." But Jacob said, "I will not let you go until you bless me." "What is your name?" the man asked. He answered, "Jacob." Then the man said, "You shall no longer be spoken of as Jacob, but as Israel, because you have contended with divine and human beings and have prevailed." Jacob then asked him, "Do tell me your name." He answered, "Why should you want to know my name?" With that, he bade him farewell. Jacob named the place Peniel, "Because I have seen God face to face," he said, "yet my life has been spared." At sunrise, as he left Penuel, Jacob limped along because of his hip. (Gen 32)

Christian Action: Today if you find yourself moving into self-pity or envy because of something you find it hard to accept, try to focus on the blessings in your life, including the blessing contained in your burden.

WEEK 6: FRIDAY

Turning Points

Life is difficult, and scarcely ever stops challenging us. But there are times when something happens that shakes us up completely, and ends by changing the course of our lives. We say goodbye to a familiar place, and move to another city. We change careers. We are seriously injured or stricken with an illness. Our marriage reaches an impasse. Our parenting days come to an end. We retire. Our world is suddenly upended.

These are all deeply challenging events. What they have in common is that one way of life is coming to an end, but the new way of life has not yet been revealed. What used to work will work no longer, but what we are supposed to do now we have no idea. In fact, we wonder if we can carry on at all. There is a crisis of meaning. We feel out of control and afraid.

Human growth happens more or less constantly, imperceptibly, as we respond to the challenges and opportunities of life. But times such as we are describing are especially significant for who we will become, for the kind of self we will create. That is because these critical junctures challenge us much more deeply. There is new learning, there is a painful stretching of our capacities, and there are crucial choices to make.

Growth, unfortunately, is not guaranteed. It comes at a price. When we come to one of these turning points, we can get stuck and stay stuck, never moving on to life's next stage. We can even regress to an earlier level of development. Or we can summon up our courage and pass over into the new. It is something like the Hebrew people in the desert, caught between two lands. They spent forty years there. Some would have stayed longer. Some wanted to go back to Egypt. Some wanted to press on, into the land of promise.

Is there a land of promise for us? Our faith says yes. A central Christian mystery is our ally at the turning points. It is the death and resurrection of Jesus. Usually we conceive it too narrowly. We think of it as something that happened just once, to him. Or we think of it as a promise touching ourselves only where our physical death is concerned. Actually, it is much broader than that. It is the key that opens up the whole meaning of our existence.

As we live we are *always* dying, and hence always afraid and in need of some assurance. We are *always* losing what we had possessed, *always* being pushed out of the familiar into the unfamiliar, *always* changing. The death/resurrection of Jesus serves as a paradigm or model for us in this ongoing experience. It consoles us because it unveils who God is for us and what God is doing for us. With God, it shows, death is never the last word. Life is. God is at work in the depth of things, laboring with us to bring life out of death, good out of evil, meaning out of absurdity. God supports us and invites us forward into a future that contains even greater good for us than the past did.

The seven sacraments of the Roman Catholic tradition bring the death/resurrection mystery of Jesus to bear on many of life's critical junctures. When some kind of death threatens and the meaning of human life is called into question, a sacramental ritual gives us the assurance we need, the pledge of God's presence and saving activity. Baptism speaks that word of assurance to our birth into a threatening world. Confirmation reiterates it for the crisis of emerging adulthood. Matrimony brings it to bear on the challenge of building a life of love together. Orders speaks it to the challenge of assuming leadership in the Christian community. Anointing declares it to the crisis of meaning entailed in serious illness. Reconciliation speaks it as needed to the crisis of broken community. The eucharist, primary maintenance sacrament of the

Christian people, reminds us on a weekly or daily basis of the death/resurrection mystery undergirding our lives.

The meaning of the great paradigm is always the same: if we join our deaths with the death of Jesus, we will also share with him in his resurrection, because God is a God of life.

Good News: Jesus said: "The hour has come for the Son of Man to be glorified. I solemnly assure you, unless the grain of wheat falls to the earth and dies, it remains just a grain of wheat. But if it dies, it produces much fruit.

"If you love your life you will lose it, while if you hate your life in this world you will preserve it to eternal life. If you would serve me you must follow me; where I am, there will my servant be. If you serve me, my Father will honor you.

"Now my soul is troubled. Yet what shall I say—Father, save me from this hour? But it was for this that I came to this hour. Father, glorify your name." (Jn 12:23-28)

Christian Action: Retrace some of the death/resurrection moments of your life. Did you experience God's fidelity? Is there some critical transition going on in your life right now? What do you think God's call to you in this situation is?

WEEK 6: SATURDAY

Wonder as Worship

Have you ever noticed a beautiful sunrise on your way to work and found yourself praising God for it? Or caught the smile on your child's face and wondered at God's creation? If you have, you have, at least for one moment, become aware of the presence of God in creation. You have been contemplative.

Prayer is something we take time out for, a specific activity.

God-awareness, contemplation, or prayerfulness is much broader. It is a way of moving through the entire day. It is an attitude, a whole approach to life. Its basis is the conviction that life is lived before God and with God. It is rooted in the realization that God is the giver of all gifts, and that God is in all things expressing self. Prayerfulness is awareness of that and responsiveness to it.

Prayerfulness does not come easily in modern society. Our ordinary attitude toward the things around us is to size them up and figure out how we can master or use them. It is a combination of technology and consumerism. It is difficult for us to move from that to a stance that just looks, and lets things be. That is what contemplation does: it looks closely, and ends in wonder.

Have you ever really *taken* a shower? To do it, you might have to remember a bygone year when you were unable to take a shower for a long time. Remember what the shower at the end of that waiting period *felt* like? Or you might have to imagine taking a shower without soap, because it is only then that you can really feel the difference the soap makes. To *take* a shower, you have to be there when it happens to you. You have to receive it.

Have you ever really *looked* at the head of cabbage you were cutting up, or really *tasted* a bowl of soup? Have you ever focused on some of the trees in your neighborhood, or watched children playing on a playground? Have you *listened* to the birds in the morning? Have you *felt* the bed you sleep in? (It helps if you have spent a night on a bus.) Have you ever thanked your car for being there when you came out? Have you thanked it for starting? G.K. Chesterton once remarked that the best way to love something is to realize that you might lose it—which is probably why people who are told they have only a short time left to live suddenly find themselves cherishing the simplest things.

The Buddhists have a word for the attitude to life I am trying to describe. They call it "mindfulness." It means really being there—present, attentive, receptive.

What do mere looking and listening, tasting and feeling have to do with prayer? Well, what is prayer? Prayer is awareness of and response to the mystery of God present. But God is the mystery in the depth of *all* things. Mindfulness or full attentiveness to things is the beginning of wonder and gratitude, and wonder and gratitude are other names for worship.

The person who wants to be prayerful seizes another kind of occasion too. There are many "dead times" of the day—when we are standing in line at the bank or grocery store, driving on the freeway, doing routine tasks like the dishes, lying in bed waiting for sleep—when we can advert to and be with the Presence. It is all part of the same attitude, that life is lived always before God and with God. On days when we cannot make time for more formal prayer, or even when we can, we can always be prayerful.

Prayerfulness, God-awareness, mindfulness, contemplation —these are just different names for an attitude of living faith.

Good News: How deep are the riches and the wisdom and the knowledge of God! How inscrutable God's judgments, how unsearchable God's ways! For "who has known the mind of the Lord? Or who has been the Lord's counselor? Who has given God anything so as to deserve return?" For from God and through God and for God all things are. To God be glory forever. Amen. (Rm 11:33–36)

Christian Action: Try today to be mindful, to receive and give thanks for the gifts of life you usually take for granted.

WEEK 6: SUNDAY

Beyond Jesus and Me

Several months had gone by since Chris' retreat. Chris was feeling discouraged with the way things were going, and took the problem to Jesus.

Chris: I don't feel very close to you, Jesus, and I'm pretty discouraged. I had a great retreat experience with you, and thought we were all set. I had never been so happy. Since then you seem pretty far away and I feel alone again.

Jesus: I'm really with you, Chris. You just can't feel me.

I'm just as much with you as I was during retreat, and I'm going to stay with you too, no matter what happens.

Chris: I sort of believe that, but it's not enough. I want so much more. I want to *feel* you and *hear* you, the way I did on retreat.

Jesus: You probably remember the gospel story of my transfiguration. We were on a mountain when it happened, and the disciples who were with me found it so wonderful they just wanted to stay there, actually to build houses there. I had to lead them down the mountain to where some needy people were. That's the problem with spiritual consolation. If you get too much of it, you forget all about the people who need your help. Often, too, you begin to think you're holier than most people.

Chris: I don't really see much danger of that. I think I would keep trying to do what is good. What I've wanted ever since I got a taste of it on retreat is some real spirituality.

Jesus: My kind of spirituality is loving people, Chris, and taking care of their needs. I know you love me. What I always used to say to people in my earthly days was: If you love me, keep my commandments. I stressed the practicality of it. An emotional religion is easier than the kind I taught. When Peter told me three times after my resurrection that he loved me (we had had a falling out), I took him very seriously. And so I asked him to feed my sheep. I wanted him to translate his love for me into love for others.

Chris: I'm trying to do that. I'm actively involved in the peace movement, for example. But I don't feel holy when I'm doing that. I just feel frustrated. It often seems we're not making any impression. And then I get mad at all the people who just can't grasp the point.

Jesus: I know what you mean, Chris. I very rarely felt holy when I was doing my work on earth either. It was extremely demanding, and I met with a lot of resistance. You saw where it all got me. Yet I knew it was what God wanted me to be about. God wouldn't let me stay in the desert, and you can see from the gospels that I never led other people into any kind of desert spirituality. We worked for the reign of God in the real world. Of course I prayed, and I enjoyed my time alone with God, but my prayer always led me back to work.

Chris: Speaking of feeling holy, even when I try to love my own family better, I don't have very good feelings about it. It's so hard. They're all good people, but sometimes they bring out the very worst in me.

Jesus: It is hard work, Chris. But I think you grow more as a person in those struggles than you do sitting in church. Sometimes religion is an escape. It is mainly in grappling with relationships that people grow. That is why I've stressed community, truth-telling, non-violence, kindness, mutual service, generosity, faithfulness, forgiveness so much. Those are the things that really test the quality of the person. That's where the growth that counts either happens or does not happen.

Chris: I'm not sure I like what you're saying, but I'm beginning to see your point. It is a lot easier to love the God we don't see than the people we do, and feeling good is more pleasant than doing good. I see where I've sometimes gotten my priorities mixed up.

Jesus: It's one of the most common spiritual mistakes. You're doing a good job, Chris. Keep doing it, and you will keep growing. Don't worry too much about the feelings. Remember that I am with you always, whether you feel it or not.

Good News: Jesus was still addressing the crowds when his mother and his brothers appeared outside to speak with him. Someone said to him, "Your mother and your brothers are standing out there and they wish to speak to you." He said to the one who had told him, "Who is my mother? Who are my brothers?" Then, extending his hand toward his disciples, he said, "There are my mother and my brothers. Whoever does the will of my heavenly Father is brother and sister and mother to me." (Mt 12:46–50)

Christian Action: Examine your faith life to see whether it revolves chiefly around religious feelings or around working for the reign of God in the world. If you would like to be doing more, take some practical steps toward that goal.